ADVANCE PRAISE

"Real and wise."

—**Jack Kornfield, PhD,** author of *After the Ecstasy, the Laundry*

"Desmond's clear, gentle writing style matches his approach to meeting our traumas and past sufferings. With his *Buddhist Practices for Healing Trauma,* he encourages readers to nurture the seeds of compassion within us, making healing within reach."

—**Sharon Salzberg,** author of *Lovingkindness* and *Real Life*

"Tim Desmond offers a clear, compassionate pathway for healing that honors both Buddhist wisdom and the realities of trauma. Structured around cycles of strengthening, acceptance, and transformation—and grounded in safety, choice, and embodied practice—this book helps practitioners build capacity without overwhelm and translate insight into compassionate action. A practical, trustworthy, and deeply humane guide."

—**David Treleaven, PhD,** author of *Trauma-Sensitive Mindfulness*

BUDDHIST
PRACTICES
for
HEALING
TRAUMA

BUDDHIST PRACTICES

for

HEALING TRAUMA

Tim Desmond

Norton Professional Books

An Imprint of W. W. Norton & Company
Independent Publishers Since 1923

Note to Readers: This book is intended as a general information resource for professionals practicing in the field of psychotherapy and mental health. It is not a substitute for appropriate training or clinical supervision. Standards of clinical practice and protocol vary in different practice settings and change over time. No technique or recommendation is guaranteed to be safe or effective in all circumstances, and neither the publisher nor the author(s) can guarantee the complete accuracy, efficacy, or appropriateness of any particular recommendation in every respect or in all settings or circumstances.

Any URLs displayed in this book link or refer to websites that existed as of press time. The publisher is not responsible for, and should not be deemed to endorse or recommend, any website other than its own or any content that it did not create. The author, also, is not responsible for any third-party material.

For information about permission to reproduce selections from this book, write to Permissions, W. W. Norton & Company, Inc., 500 Fifth Avenue, New York, NY 10110

For information about special discounts for bulk purchases, please contact W. W. Norton Special Sales at specialsales@wwnorton.com or 800-233-4830

Manufacturing by Versa Press
Book design by Anna Knighton
Production manager: Gwen Cullen

ISBN: 978-1-324-08247-7 (Paperback)

W. W. Norton & Company, Inc., 500 Fifth Avenue, New York, NY 10110
www.wwnorton.com

W. W. Norton & Company Ltd., 15 Carlisle Street, London W1D 3BS

Authorized EU representative: EAS, Mustamäe tee 50, 10621 Tallinn, Estonia

1 2 3 4 5 6 7 8 9 0

*This book is dedicated to our spiritual ancestors
who forged the path of healing, and to our descendants
who we might make the world better for.*

CONTENTS

FIRST CYCLE

Contents

SECOND CYCLE

THIRD CYCLE

FOURTH CYCLE

Contents

ACKNOWLEDGMENTS

Everything I've learned about how to transform suffering and cultivate joy in myself and others I have learned from Thich Nhat Hanh, the monks and nuns of Plum Village, and the other spiritual teachers I've been fortunate enough to meet. I can't thank them enough.

I also feel deep gratitude for the support and encouragement I've received from mentors and friends, especially Joanne Friday, Richie Davidson, Tara Brach, and Larry Boyang. Thank you to Johanna Hoffman for the inspiring conversations that helped clarify and organize these teachings.

All of the people at W. W. Norton have been incredibly helpful in bringing this book into existence. Thanks so much for your guidance and support in this project.

To my wonderful son Finnegan, thank you for being such an inspiration and source of love in the world.

WHAT IS TRAUMA?
A BUDDHIST APPROACH

Trauma is garbage.

Yet, as any good gardener knows, *garbage* can be transformed into *compost*. And compost is an indispensable resource for a healthy garden. Compost, too, can be transformed. When used skillfully, it becomes beautiful flowers and healthy vegetables. Compost stinks at first, but it also brings life into your garden.

Just like garbage, trauma can be transformed. It can become the qualities of compassion, resilience, joy, and a new appreciation for life. As we learn how to embrace our pain with love and radical acceptance, our heart opens. We are not only more resilient in the face of future challenges, but more capable of helping others. Transforming trauma is not easy but it is possible. This book walks you through the process.

In Buddhism, we learn three types of practices for transforming trauma. First, there are *strengthening practices* that help us develop enough stability and love to be present with our trauma without being overwhelmed by it. Second, there are *acceptance practices* that help us make contact with our trauma and give ourselves space to experience all of our feelings. Third, there are *transformative practices* to actually heal our trauma in the present moment. While only the transformative practices engage directly with trauma, all three types are important, and they work together to create healing.

This book is made up of small sections—just a few pages each—that contain one concrete practice or teaching. We start with some strengthening practices, move to acceptance, and then transformative practices. We repeat that cycle a total of four times, each time revisiting the teachings from a new angle and deepening the learning. As you progress through these four cycles, the pattern of strengthening, acceptance, and transformation will feel more and more natural.

Additionally, each cycle includes sutra study, in which we explore traditional Buddhist teachings and their relationship to our path of healing. Finally, each cycle ends with compassionate action. Those sections allow us to complete the process of garbage to compost to flowers by allowing some of the healing we've experienced to become energy and action for the benefit of others.

Some of the sections in this book will feel like totally new ways of looking at trauma. Others might seem simple or obvious. The goal of this book is not to prepare you for your PhD. It is to help you heal. Some practices that are simple to understand are not easy to do. The strengthening and acceptance practices prepare you, so that when you come to the transforming practices, you'll be ready to benefit as deeply as possible. If you are more experienced at working with your trauma, feel free to skip around.

After finishing a section, I encourage you to stop reading and take some time to reflect on what you've read. If you encounter a new idea or practice, reflect on what it would be like to take that idea to its logical conclusion. What would it be like if you truly adopted this new way of thinking? Which situations in your life would be easy places to apply this teaching, and which would be challenging or even inappropriate? How could you rephrase or even change the teaching so that it would be a better fit in your life?

SAFETY AND OVERWHELM

As you engage with these practices, be gentle with yourself. Trauma has a tendency to overwhelm us, and that's not helpful for healing. On this journey, pay attention to the level of emotional intensity in your body. Ideally, you want to keep the level of intensity you're feeling between 3 and 7 out of 10. Below 3 means the practice is too superficial to be very helpful. Above 7 means the emotion is too big to hold with compassion.

As you move through this book, if you find yourself at an 8 or above, stop and bring your attention to some of the objects in the room where you're reading. Look around, feel your feet on the ground, and maybe move your body. Then you can go to one of the strengthening practices to recharge.

THE GARDEN OF THE MIND: UNDERSTANDING TRAUMA THROUGH EMOTIONAL SEEDS

Buddhism uses countless analogies in its teachings, particularly analogies to agricultural life and the natural world. In addition to the image of suffering as compost, another Buddhist teaching describes suffering as a type of *seed (bīja)* in a garden.

In this teaching, all emotions are seen as seeds in the garden of our minds. If we can understand the nature of this garden and how to care for it, we'll gain insight into our trauma and how to heal. Each of us carries within ourselves the potential for a vast array of emotions—joy, sorrow, anger, love, fear, and curiosity—all of which exist as dormant seeds waiting for the right conditions to sprout.

Imagine a magic garden with countless types of seeds lying beneath the soil. There is a seed of anger, a seed of joy, a seed of concentration, and many others. Each seed requires specific conditions in order to sprout. For example, if it's very hot and dry, the seed of anger will sprout in the garden. If it's cold and dark, the seed of sadness will sprout. When the sky is clear with a gentle breeze, the seed of joy will sprout. There's a seed for every possible mental state waiting in the soil of this garden, and the conditions in the environment determine which ones will come to life for us to experience.

The conditions in this garden are always changing. A seed might sprout up and manifest for an hour or so, but when the conditions change, it returns to its seed form under the soil, waiting for another chance to manifest. A weather system might pass through causing the seed of curiosity to sprout and bloom. When the weather changes, curiosity returns to the soil as a seed.

HOW TRAUMA SHAPES THE GARDEN

One of the unusual aspects of this magic garden is that every time a seed sprouts, it becomes stronger. If the conditions in the garden repeatedly favor fear or anger, those seeds will grow more robust, making them more likely to sprout again in the future. Over time, these seeds may grow into towering trees, overshadowing the rest of the garden, dominating our emotional landscape.

This is how trauma manifests in the mind. The seed of suffering, once small, may have been watered again and again—through painful experiences, conditioned responses, and habitual thoughts—until it has grown into a massive tree with deep roots. Whether through a single life-altering event or the accumulation of many painful moments, the seed of suffering becomes so strong that it arises even with the slightest provocation. The mind becomes conditioned to expect suffering; perceiving danger where none exists; reacting with fear, anger, or withdrawal at the smallest trigger.

CULTIVATING LOVING-AWARENESS: THE KEY TO HEALING

The most important secret of the magic garden is the presence of a special seed called loving-awareness. Some call it mindfulness, others self-compassion, but regardless of its name, it holds the power to heal. When loving-awareness sprouts and blooms, it releases a powerful fragrance that permeates the entire garden. This fragrance has a calming effect, soothing even the tallest tree of suffering. Over time, as loving-awareness continues to bloom alongside suffering, it weakens the seed of suffering, making it less likely to sprout unnecessarily.

Healing from trauma is not about eradicating certain seeds from our garden—it is about cultivating the seeds that nourish peace, resilience, and wisdom. If we continuously water the seed of loving-awareness, it will grow stronger, allowing us to meet our suffering with understanding rather than resistance.

Through Buddhist practice, we learn how to:

1. *Recognize when our seed of suffering has been activated.* By bringing mindful attention to our emotions, we can see when fear, anger, or grief is arising.

2. *Stop reinforcing the seed of suffering.* When we react from trauma, we inadvertently strengthen the pattern. Instead, we can pause, breathe, and create space between stimulus and response.

3. *Water the seeds of healing.* By consciously nurturing mindfulness, self-compassion, and joy, we strengthen these qualities, making them more available in difficult moments.

4. *Use loving-awareness to transform suffering.* When your seed of loving-awareness is strong enough, you will invite your suffering to manifest while holding it with loving-awareness. *The contact between these two seeds is transformative and has the capacity to change your life.*

TRAUMA AS EMERGENCY LEARNING

A third analogy that can help us understand trauma is to see it as a special form of learning. Trauma often feels like being stuck in the past, but that's not actually what's happening. Instead, we can view trauma as a form of *emergency learning*: a deeply ingrained survival mechanism designed to protect us from future danger. When faced with a seriously threatening situation, the brain and body shift into a heightened state of awareness, paying attention to every possible detail that could be associated with the threat. For example, in a car crash, the brain might associate cars with danger, but it also might associate whatever you were smelling, thinking about, or the weather that day. The brain is looking for anything that could possibly predict future danger, and in this state it doesn't want to miss anything.

Once this emergency learning takes place, anything remotely connected to that original experience can trigger a full-body defense response. Your nervous system prepares you for another life-threatening event. This is why trauma survivors often feel as though we are reliving our worst moments, even when we are physically safe. Our brains and bodies are determined not to miss any clue that another life-threatening experience might be imminent. The trauma response is not a failure of the mind but an adaptation aimed at survival.

From this perspective, healing also includes the process of retraining your mind to distinguish between stimuli that could predict a real threat, and those that don't. When we've developed enough loving-awareness to stay grounded, we reexamine old memories in order to improve what we can learn from the experience. Often, some of the most powerful moments in healing trauma go along with recognizing a change in what the original experience *meant about you or the world.*

HOW TRAUMA FEEDS ANXIETY AND DEPRESSION

Trauma doesn't just live in our memories—it shapes the entire way we experience the world. For many of us, the effects of trauma show up not only as flashbacks or nightmares but as chronic anxiety or depression as well. When we carry unresolved trauma, our nervous systems stay on alert, scanning for danger that may no longer be present. This can lead to persistent anxiety, restlessness, or difficulty trusting that we're safe. At the same time, trauma can create a sense of helplessness or disconnection, leaving us feeling numb, hopeless, or unworthy—hallmarks of depression.

In Buddhist terms, if trauma means our seed of suffering is very strong, that suffering can take the form of fear or despair. If we don't know how to meet that suffering with compassion and clarity, we get stuck. Anxiety and depression aren't separate from trauma; they are often the most common and enduring shapes it can take.

THE PATH TO TRANSFORMATION

Thankfully, Buddhist psychology's main focus is the healing and transformation of suffering. Trauma is not a life sentence; it is a conditioned pattern that can be changed. Through the practices in this book, you will learn how to cultivate the garden of your mind with intention. You will explore how to stop strengthening the seed of suffering and how to use loving-awareness to heal your wounds at the deepest level.

Just as no storm lasts forever, no suffering is permanent. With patience and practice, we can transform even the most deeply rooted patterns of trauma. We can create a garden where loving-awareness grows abundantly, providing shade and refuge for all the seeds within us. As we nurture this practice, we find that healing is not about eliminating difficult emotions but about creating the right conditions for peace, joy, and resilience to flourish.

CONCLUSION

Trauma is not just something that happens to individuals; it is woven into the collective human experience. In Buddhist thought, suffering is universal, and so is the capacity for awakening. By integrating insights from psychology and Buddhist philosophy, we gain a more holistic understanding of trauma—one that neither pathologizes nor diminishes it, but instead offers a way through.

Through mindfulness, compassion, and wisdom, we can learn to meet our suffering not as a prison but as a gateway to greater understanding and freedom. This book is about that journey: how we can use Buddhist practice to transform trauma, reclaim our sense of wholeness, and walk the path toward healing and liberation.

BUDDHIST
PRACTICES
for
HEALING
TRAUMA

FIRST
CYCLE

ENJOYING
THE BREATH
STRENGTHENING

In Latin and Sanskrit, as well as many other languages, the word for breath also means "the energy of life." In Latin, the word *spiritus* means both breath and spirit. In Sanskrit, the word *prana* means both breath and the vital energy that animates all living beings. When the Buddha taught people to bring their attention to the breath, the word he used also had this added meaning. As you breathe, it's possible to feel the energy of life flowing through you. The breath is not merely air entering and leaving the body—it is a wave of vitality, always available to refresh and restore us.

In each moment of life, your breath is available. It is unique in that it happens on its own, but it's also easily controlled. This dual nature makes it a great object for learning to meditate.

For those of us healing from trauma, the breath can become a powerful ally. Trauma often causes the mind and body to feel disconnected or trapped in past distress. By turning attention to the breath, we come home to the present moment, where we can find freedom and safety. Mindful breathing has the ability to calm the mind, and it is also a profound way to nurture joy and resilience in everyday life. If we can learn to find enjoyment in the simple act of breathing, then we have access to a source of energy and renewal no matter what difficulties arise.

COMING HOME TO THE BREATH

Many of us live in a state of mental restlessness. Our thoughts race toward the future or pull us back into the past, often reinforcing the pain of trauma. But the breath is always in the present. When we bring our full awareness to the breath, we return home to ourselves. This home is not found in a particular place but in the feeling of being present and at ease in our own body.

A simple way to begin enjoying the breath is to notice it without trying to change it. Find a comfortable position—sitting, standing, or lying down—and gently close your eyes if that feels safe. Bring your attention to the natural rhythm of your breath, feeling the air move in and out of your body. Is your breath deep or shallow? Fast or slow? Simply observe with curiosity and kindness. Let it be however it wants to be.

Now, try offering yourself a simple phrase with each breath. As you inhale, silently say, "Breathing in, I know I am breathing in." As you exhale, say, "Breathing out, I know I am breathing out." This simple acknowledgment strengthens mindfulness, allowing the breath to become more vivid and enjoyable. This is the practice of allowing the world to be exactly as it is in the present moment.

THE BREATH AS A SOURCE OF JOY

In Buddhist mindfulness practice, the breath is not merely a tool for relaxation or concentration—it can be a deep well of happiness. The Buddha taught that when we breathe mindfully, we can experience a lightness of being, a natural joy that arises from simple awareness.

One way to experience this is through gentle smiling. Try bringing a soft smile to your lips as you breathe. Notice how this small action changes your experience of the breath. A smile signals to the body that it is safe, encouraging the release of tension. It is like offering kindness to yourself with each inhale and exhale.

Another practice is to focus on the breath as the energy of life moving through you. Try silently saying, "Breathing in, I am alive. Breathing out, I smile to life." You can change those words, or abandon them if they don't feel helpful. This simple practice can transform the breath into something delightful. Over time, as we learn to associate the breath with ease and happiness, it becomes a reliable refuge in difficult moments.

USING THE BREATH TO SOOTHE THE BODY

Trauma is often stored in the body, manifesting as tension, discomfort, or a sense of unease. Because our breath is directly connected to our nervous system, mindful breathing can help release this weight we carry.

Another practice to try is deep belly breathing. Place a hand on your abdomen and take a slow, deep breath, allowing the belly to rise as you inhale and fall as you exhale. This kind of breathing activates the vagus nerve and other elements of the parasympathetic nervous system, signaling to the body that it is safe. With each deep breath, visualize tension leaving the body, like a wave washing away stress.

You can also experiment with a four–six breathing pattern. Inhale to a slow count of four, then exhale to a slow count of six. The extended exhale helps to calm the heart rate and reduce feelings of anxiety. As you do this, imagine each breath carrying a sense of warmth and comfort, gently dissolving any areas of tightness or pain.

BREATH AS A SAFE ANCHOR
IN DIFFICULT MOMENTS

When trauma surfaces, it can feel overwhelming, as if we are being pulled out of the present moment into a storm of emotions. In these times, the breath can serve as an anchor, keeping us connected to the here and now.

In moments of overwhelm, a helpful practice can be to whisper a phrase of reassurance with each breath. For example:

○ "Breathing in, I am safe."

○ "Breathing out, I am loved."

By pairing the breath with comforting words, we reinforce a sense of security and self-compassion. Even in the midst of emotional turmoil, we can return to this simple rhythm and find steadiness.

INTEGRATING ENJOYABLE BREATHING INTO DAILY LIFE

The beauty of breath awareness is that it can be practiced anywhere, at any time. Whether sitting in meditation, walking, or engaging in daily tasks, the breath is always with us.

See if you can weave small moments of mindful breathing into your routine. When waking up, take a few conscious breaths before getting out of bed. Before eating, take a slow breath to arrive fully in the present moment. When feeling stressed, pause for three deep breaths before doing anything. These small moments build a habit of presence, making mindful breathing a natural refuge in daily life.

Your breath is available in every moment of your life. If you can learn how to make it a source of joy, then you have access to a powerful source of energy when life feels difficult. Trauma may create patterns of tension and fear, but the breath remains a steady companion, always offering an opportunity for renewal. Through gentle attention and appreciation, the breath can become a path to healing, resilience, and inner peace.

2

HERE
AND NOW
STRENGTHENING

Right now, as you read this book, you are safe. It's true that you weren't always safe in the past, and you won't always be safe in the future. But in this present moment, right now, you are safe. Your body is here, supported by the ground beneath you. Your breath moves in and out, a steady rhythm that reminds you that you're alive. Right now, nothing is threatening you.

One of the most important elements of healing trauma is learning how to feel safe when you are safe. If you're in danger, your body's natural survival instincts—fear, anger, or a heightened sense of alertness—are appropriate responses. They prepare you to fight, flee, or hide. But for many of us who have experienced trauma, these responses don't turn off when the danger is gone. Instead, we live in a constant state of readiness, as if the threat never ended. The body and mind continue to brace for impact long after the impact has passed.

This is where the practice of coming home to the present moment becomes essential. The present moment is always available to us. It is the only moment in which we can truly live. Learning to recognize a safe moment as a safe moment gives our sympathetic nervous system—the part of us that activates our threat response—a chance to rest, and allows us to settle into a more peaceful state.

RECOGNIZING THE PRESENT MOMENT AS SAFE

One of the key skills in healing trauma is being able to distinguish between past danger and present safety. The mind is often trapped in old stories, playing back memories as it scans for any possible sign of danger. These memories can trigger emotional and physical reactions as if the past were happening all over again. Similarly, the mind projects into the future, creating scenarios of worry and fear that make us feel unsafe even when nothing is wrong.

A critical practice in healing is pausing to ask, "Am I safe right now?" If you look around and see that there is no immediate danger, take a deep breath and remind yourself: *In this moment, I am safe. I can allow myself to feel safe, for just this moment.* This does not mean dismissing past trauma or ignoring legitimate concerns about the future. It means allowing yourself the opportunity to experience the reality of now, which is often much safer than the mind assumes.

PRACTICES FOR RETURNING TO THE HERE AND NOW

There are many ways to come home to the present moment. Each of these practices can serve as an anchor, a way to gently return your attention to the here and now. Try each of them, and notice which ones resonate with you.

1. Anchoring in the Breath

Your breath is always in the present moment. Unlike thoughts, which can drift to the past or future, the breath only exists in the here and now.

Try this:

○ Take a slow inhale, noticing the feeling of the air entering your nostrils.

○ Pause briefly at the top of the breath, feeling the fullness of your lungs.

○ Exhale gently, following the sensation of the air leaving your body.

○ Continue for a few minutes, allowing the rhythm of the breath to steady you.

○ You might add the word "here" to your in-breath, and the word "now" to your out-breath.

Each inhale is a reminder that you are alive. Each exhale is an opportunity to release tension. If your mind drifts to old fears or future worries, gently bring your attention back to the breath.

2. Feeling the Sensations in the Body

The body is another anchor that connects you to the present moment. Trauma often disconnects us from bodily sensations, making us feel as though we are floating outside of ourselves. Reconnecting with the body helps us feel grounded and real.

Try this:

○ Place your hands on your lap, your heart, or on a solid surface.

○ Notice the feeling of your feet on the ground.

○ Scan your body, moving your awareness from head to toe, noticing any sensations—warmth, coolness, tingling, pressure.

○ If you find tension or discomfort, give it permission to exist and be willing to feel it. You might speak to that tension and say, "I'm here for you, and you don't need to go away."

○ If that tension wants to relax, that's great. If not, just practice learning how to be open to an uncomfortable feeling and give yourself the gift of acceptance.

By turning attention to the body, you reinforce the message that you are here, now.

3. Watching the Mind With Curiosity

The mind is constantly moving, pulling us into stories of the past or predictions about the future. Mindfulness teaches us that we don't have to believe every thought that arises. Instead, we can observe thoughts like clouds passing through the sky—acknowledging them without becoming entangled.

Try this:

- Close your eyes and take a few slow breaths.

- Notice the thoughts that come and go without trying to change them.

- If a thought pulls you in, gently say to yourself, "This is a thought," and return to your breath or body.

- Imagine each thought drifting away like a leaf floating on a stream.

- It's okay for thoughts to be persistent. You don't need to make any thoughts go away. You just recognize "I'm here in the present moment, and I'm thinking about the past (or present, or future)." This helps you learn to distinguish between thoughts and reality.

This practice helps you notice when your thoughts are pulling you away from the reality of the present. We don't try to stop our thinking. We just learn to recognize a thought as a thought, rather than confusing it for reality itself. With time, you learn to recognize these mental patterns and return to reality in the present.

GIVING THE NERVOUS SYSTEM
A CHANCE TO REST

When we spend much of our time in a state of hypervigilance, our nervous system never fully relaxes. Over time, this can lead to exhaustion, anxiety, and physical symptoms, such as headaches, digestive issues, and muscle pain. By learning to recognize safety when it's present, we help the nervous system shift from survival mode into a state of rest and repair.

One way to facilitate this shift is through the *three-breath pause*:

1. Take a deep inhale, feeling the air enter your lungs.

2. Hold for a moment, feeling your body settle.
   Try saying, "Safe here."

3. Exhale slowly, allowing any tension to release.
   Try saying, "Safe now."

4. Repeat two more times, letting each breath be slower and softer.

This simple practice signals to the body that it is safe. Over time, moments of peace become easier to access.

MAKING THE PRESENT MOMENT A HOME

Coming home to the present moment is not just a technique—it can be a way of life. We can teach the body and mind that not every moment has to be filled with fear or tension. We can reclaim our sense of safety and peace, even in small moments throughout the day.

As you continue reading, pause every so often and remind yourself: *Right now, I am safe.* Take a breath, feel your body, and let the truth of this moment settle in. Over time, this simple act of returning to now can transform the way you experience life.

The present moment is always here, always available. Learning to rest in the now is one of the most profound gifts you can give yourself. It allows your body to heal, your mind to settle, and your heart to find peace. Trauma may have conditioned you to live in fear, but you are not bound to that experience forever. With each breath, with each moment of awareness, you are building a new home—one rooted in presence, safety, and peace.

3

EMOTIONS AS SENSATION IN THE BODY
STRENGTHENING

Our emotions are deeply physical experiences that are rooted in the body. Whether we feel joy, fear, anger, or sadness, these emotions manifest as sensations—warmth, tightness, shakiness, or pressure—within us. Learning to relate to our emotions as physical sensations allows us to navigate them with greater ease, and to care for them when that's what they need.

UNDERSTANDING POSITIVE EMOTIONS AS A GIFT

What we often call "positive emotions"—joy, love, gratitude, contentment—are a gift from our body and brain. These emotions arise as signals, letting us know that we are meeting our needs in a good way. They encourage us to continue along paths that lead to well-being and connection.

In Buddhism, we distinguish between wholesome and unwholesome pleasures. A *wholesome pleasure* is one that brings happiness in the present and also contributes to more happiness in the future. Examples include acts of kindness, mindful appreciation of beauty, or deep, meaningful relationships. An *unwholesome pleasure*, on the other hand, provides temporary happiness but leads to suffering in the future, such as overindulging in food or engaging in other harmful behaviors for immediate gratification. From this perspective, we can allow ourselves to completely enjoy wholesome pleasures. At the same time, we seek to avoid unwholesome pleasures out of a simple understanding that they will cause future suffering, rather than from any sense of moral judgment.

By recognizing positive emotions as sensations in the body, we can fully experience them without clinging to them. Just as a pleasant breeze can be enjoyed but not grasped, emotions, too, come and go. By simply noticing them and allowing them to be, we cultivate a sense of gratitude and openness to joy.

UNDERSTANDING NEGATIVE EMOTIONS AS A GIFT

Negative emotions are not mistakes or weaknesses; they are also a gift from our body and brain. They are part of our *threat-response system*, alerting us to potential harm and eliciting responses that may help us navigate threats.

Broadly, negative emotions fall into three main categories:

1. *Fear*, which helps us avoid a threat.

2. *Anger*, which helps us confront a threat.

3. *Grief*, which helps us solicit help from others.

Each of these emotions has played a crucial role in human survival, allowing us to respond to danger, set boundaries, and seek support when in distress. However, when our *seed of suffering* has been watered repeatedly—through trauma, stress, or chronic worry—our threat-response system can become overly sensitive. This means that the smallest reminders of past harm or vague uncertainties about the future can activate powerful fear, anger, or grief, even when there is no actual danger in the present moment.

WHEN THE THREAT-RESPONSE SYSTEM BECOMES TOO SENSITIVE

When our threat-response system is activated too often, it can become overwhelming. It's like living in a home with a smoke alarm that's always going off. We might react with fear or anger when no real danger is present, or sadness might linger long after a difficult experience has passed. This heightened sensitivity can lead to unintentional harm—we may lash out at loved ones, withdraw from others, or feel stuck in cycles of suffering.

While it can be frustrating to feel overwhelmed by emotions, rejecting or suppressing them doesn't help. Instead, our key to transforming suffering is the *seed of loving-awareness*. This seed allows us to meet our emotions with understanding and compassion rather than resistance or self-judgment. If we hate our emotions and wish them away, we only create more tension. But if we meet them with patience and acceptance, we begin to cultivate inner peace.

BEGIN BY ACCEPTING YOUR EMOTIONAL STATE

The foundation of emotional healing is *acceptance*. Whatever you feel in this moment—whether pleasant or unpleasant—is real. It is happening. Rather than pushing it away, try to simply *be with it*.

In Buddhist psychology, emotions are understood as composed of two main elements:

1. *Physical sensations*. The bodily experience of the emotion—tightness in the chest, warmth in the face, trembling in the limbs.

2. *A tendency to think a certain way*. The mind naturally forms thoughts that match the emotion. For example, fear brings thoughts of worst-case scenarios, anger brings justifications for confrontation, and grief brings thoughts of loss.

Rather than getting lost in the mental storyline of an emotion, we can shift our focus to its *physical expression* in the body. This simple practice helps us relate to emotions with greater clarity and less overwhelm.

PRACTICING PRESENCE WITH EMOTIONS

1. Recognizing Emotions as Sensations

The next time you experience a strong emotion, pause and observe:

- Where do you feel it in your body?

- Is it heavy or light? Warm or cool? Moving or still?

- Can you simply allow the sensation to be there without trying to change it? It might not feel good, but see if it's tolerable.

By identifying emotions as bodily sensations rather than being lost in their stories, you create space to respond with wisdom rather than react impulsively.

2. Allowing Emotions to Be

If fear is present, it doesn't necessarily mean you're in danger. It simply means that a part of you wants to prepare for a possible threat. If anger is present, it doesn't mean you have to fight—it means that part of you perceives a boundary being crossed.

Try saying to yourself:

- "Fear is here. That's okay. I feel it in my chest and shoulders."

- "Anger is here. That's okay. I feel heat in my face and hands."

○ "Sadness is here. That's okay. I feel heaviness in my heart
and throat."

In this practice, we're acknowledging our emotions without resistance, allowing them to naturally arise and pass away.

3. Checking for Present Safety

When strong emotions arise, try asking yourself: "Am I safe right now?" More often than not, the answer will be yes. You'll notice that the bodily sensation of suffering is present right now, but the danger belongs to an imagined future, or a memory.

This gentle reminder can help reassure your nervous system that while the emotion is real, the danger it anticipates is not necessarily present. It is possible to allow a strong feeling of fear to exist in your body while reminding yourself that there is no real danger in the present moment.

If you feel overwhelmed, try grounding yourself:

○ Take a slow, deep breath.

○ Feel your feet firmly on the ground.

○ Notice the environment around you—the colors,
the sounds, the feeling of air on your skin.

By anchoring in the present, you help your body recognize that it is safe.

Your emotions—whether positive or negative—are not mistakes. They are gifts from your body, guiding you away from harm and toward meeting your needs. By learning to feel emotions as sensations rather than as absolute realities, greater resilience and inner peace become possible. The more you practice accepting and observing your emotions, the more freedom you will find. Over time, the habit of resisting and reacting will transform into one of awareness and gentle presence. This is the path of healing—one breath, one sensation, one moment at a time.

4

UNLOCKING NATURAL COMPASSION
STRENGTHENING

Compassion is not something we need to force or fabricate—it's an innate quality and an essential part of our human nature. However, for many of us, life experiences, trauma, and conditioning have created barriers that obscure this natural capacity. The good news is that compassion can be rediscovered and strengthened. Just as a muscle becomes stronger with consistent use, the ability to feel and express compassion grows as we engage in practices that cultivate it.

THE CARE CIRCUIT:
THE BIOLOGY OF COMPASSION

As mammals, our brains are wired for compassion and care. Neuroscientists have found that every mammal's brain contains a well-defined structure they call our care circuit, the system responsible for care giving and receiving behaviors. Every time an adult responds to a crying baby with gentleness and support, the care circuit in their brain is active. This circuit produces oxytocin, natural opiates, and other signaling chemicals that create feelings of warmth and love. It is also one of the most powerful tools in our biology for relieving distress.

The care circuit is not limited to grand acts of selflessness—it arises in simple moments, like offering a kind word, comforting a friend, or feeling tenderness toward an animal.

For those of us who've experienced trauma, this circuit may become less active or overshadowed by the brain's threat-response system. This is why, at times, compassion can feel distant or difficult to access. Fortunately, with deliberate practice, we can strengthen our capacity for compassion and unlock its natural presence within us. Then we can use this capacity to regulate our distress.

TRAINING THE MIND TO
CULTIVATE COMPASSION

Just as we train our bodies through exercise, we can train our minds to be more compassionate. The first step is recognizing that compassion is always available, even if it feels dormant. By engaging in deliberate practices, we can bring it forward and make it a more natural response in our daily lives.

One of the simplest and most effective methods for this is *sending compassion* to another being. By visualizing someone or something we care about and silently wishing them well, we activate the neural pathways associated with care and connection. Over time, this practice can expand beyond our loved ones, as we extend our practice of compassion to strangers, and even those who cause problems in our lives.

Another effective approach is consciously *receiving compassion*. For some people, it's easier to receive compassion from ourselves. For others, it's easier to visualize receiving it from someone else. I suggest that you try the practices below and see what feels the easiest and most powerful for you.

SENDING PRACTICE

O Find a comfortable position. Let your body settle. Take a few slow, deep breaths.

O See if you can visualize someone or something that brings up an *easy, uncomplicated feeling of warmth and love*. It can be a baby, an animal, or anything at all.

O Make that image as clear as possible in your mind.

O Silently say to them (changing the phrases as appropriate):
  o "May you be safe."
  o "May you be happy."
  o "May you be healthy."
  o "May you live with ease."

O Repeat these phrases slowly and gently, allowing their meaning to land. If it feels right, visualize them receiving your care—softening, smiling, or relaxing.

○ If anything challenging comes up, change the visualization to make it easier. We're looking for the easiest image that can turn on your care circuit.

○ After a few minutes, you might try expanding the circle to:
  ○ Others you love
  ○ Neutral people
  ○ People you find difficult
  ○ All beings everywhere

○ However, if anything feels challenging, go back to what was easy. This is a practice of finding the easiest route to access the energy of compassion within you, and then seeing how to turn that energy up as high as possible.

RECEIVING PRACTICE

○ Sit quietly and take a few deep breaths. Place a hand on your heart or wherever it feels soothing.

○ Bring to mind someone (real or imagined) who you feel could completely love and accept you. This could be a grandparent, spiritual figure, beloved friend, or even your future self. Anyone or anything.

○ Picture them looking at you with love. Imagine them saying:
  ○ "May you be happy."
  ○ "May you be healthy."
  ○ "May you be safe."
  ○ "May you be loved."

○ Try to receive these words into your body. Let them land like sunlight on your skin. Allow them to permeate you and envelop anywhere in your body that needs love—any tension or agitation. If resistance arises, that's okay. Welcome the part of you that is resisting, and say, "It's okay you're here. You need love too."

○ If helpful, imagine this compassion as a warm light or gentle presence surrounding and filling your body.

○ You can also speak directly to yourself in that same voice:
  o "I see how much you're hurting."
  o "I'm here for you."
  o "You are lovable, even in your suffering."

○ Stay with this practice for a few minutes or as long as it feels nourishing. You don't need to force anything. We're looking for what feels easy.

For some people, sending will feel easier, and receiving will be easier for others. Continue to practice whatever is easiest for you.

RECONNECTING WITH COMPASSION AFTER TRAUMA

For those of us who've endured trauma, compassion can feel elusive, especially toward ourselves. Past wounds may have taught us that the world is unsafe, making it difficult to trust or open our hearts. However, healing is possible. Compassion itself is a pathway to recovery.

A vital step in this process is *recognizing that self-compassion is not weakness*. Many people who've experienced trauma develop a harsh inner critic as a way to protect themselves from future harm. This voice might criticize or belittle, believing that self-judgment prevents vulnerability, or believing that the only way to explain why the trauma happened is to blame ourselves. But it's always possible to transform this voice through the practice of self-compassion.

Practicing self-compassion after trauma involves creating a safe internal environment. This can be done by engaging in small acts of kindness toward oneself, such as allowing space for rest, seeking supportive relationships, or simply acknowledging pain without self-condemnation. Over time, as compassion becomes more familiar, the nervous system begins to associate kindness with safety rather than danger.

RETURNING TO OUR TRUE NATURE

Compassion is an intrinsic part of who we are. While trauma, stress, and social conditioning may obscure it, compassion is always within reach. By engaging in practices that activate and strengthen the care circuit, we reconnect with our ability to care deeply for ourselves and others.

Over time, our basic orientation when confronted with suffering (inside ourselves or outside) can shift from avoidance and defensiveness to a posture of care. As this happens, compassion becomes a core part of our lives.

5

THE
PEACE TREATY
ACCEPTANCE

When (my seed of suffering) manifests,
I am committed not to say or do anything.

—Fourteen Mindfulness Trainings of the
Order of Interbeing, Thich Nhat Hanh

Going back to the image of the garden of our minds, we remember that trauma can be understood in terms of our seed of suffering having been watered so many times or so deeply that it has become very strong. From this perspective, it's vital that we learn how to stop watering that seed and making it stronger.

The practice of the peace treaty is the practice of recognizing when our seed of suffering has been activated and being committed not to do anything that might make it stronger. We know that every time we speak or act when motivated by our trauma, those responses become more deeply ingrained and our trauma becomes a more powerful force in our lives. If we can refrain from letting our trauma control our actions, then we've taken a major step toward preventing it from getting stronger.

RECOGNIZING THE SEED OF SUFFERING

Each of us carries seeds of both joy and suffering. Depending on our past experiences, some seeds are more easily activated than others. When the seed of suffering arises—whether in the form of irritation, sadness, fear, or anger—it's crucial that we notice it as soon as possible. If we are not mindful, our suffering will quickly dictate our actions, leading us to speak and behave in ways that escalate our pain.

Learning to recognize when our seed of suffering is active is much easier said than done. We might know that we have a strong seed of suffering, and we might know that very small causes can create powerful responses within us. However, when suffering is actually present, it can make us believe that our responses have nothing to do with our strong seed. Our suffering can make us think that the present situation is 100% responsible for our reaction. We have to learn to pay attention to our bodily sensations in order to notice when our seed of suffering is beginning to arise.

When trauma arises in the mind and body, it changes how we view the world. Small conflicts can seem like serious threats. A benign misunderstanding can seem like willful hostility. When trauma hijacks our perceptions, the world becomes unfriendly. Moreover, every minute that we inhabit such a perception of the world, that worldview becomes more solid and seems more real.

HOW TO AVOID WATERING OUR
SEED OF SUFFERING

When we recognize that the seed of suffering in us is strong, we must change how we relate to ourselves. Once we see its presence, we must develop a healthy skepticism toward our habitual reactions. This means understanding that when the seed of suffering is activated, it will naturally make us believe that we're living in a dangerous and hostile world. If we don't become aware of this cycle, it will continue to guide our perceptions, emotions, and behaviors, reinforcing our suffering.

DISARMING THE SEED OF SUFFERING

To truly disarm the seed of suffering within ourselves, we must cultivate the ability to step back from our automatic reactions. The strongest habits of mind are not easy to unlearn, and resisting the pull of suffering requires steady awareness. The key lies in learning to observe our internal landscape without immediately reacting. When suffering is present, it distorts our perception, making everything appear more threatening, urgent, or hopeless than it really is. If we act from that place of distortion, we reinforce our suffering instead of healing it.

The first step in disarming suffering is to recognize its physiological signals. Suffering doesn't just exist as a thought—it manifests in the body as tension, heaviness, agitation, and so on. When our seed of suffering is present, we can feel it in our shoulders, stomach, jaw, or chest. If we can notice these sensations as they arise, we can recognize that our perception is likely being shaped by our seed of suffering.

BREAKING THE CYCLE OF REACTIVITY

When we notice that suffering is present in our body, the most important thing we can do is to *pause*. Do not speak or act. Instead, take a deep breath, return to the present moment, and allow yourself the space to simply observe. Feel the sensations in your body and breathe. This isn't repression—it's wisdom. You are not trying to pretend that you feel differently, or forcing yourself to act dishonestly. Instead, you're acknowledging the reality of the present moment. You are fully accepting your emotions without letting them run rampant.

CAUGHT BY SUFFERING	REPRESSING SUFFERING	PEACE TREATY
We believe our emotions are being caused entirely by present circumstances. Or we recognize that we're triggered, but still speak and act while suffering is strong.	We realize that we are suffering, and we try to hide it or deny it. We might try to force ourselves to feel differently, and feel angry or ashamed when we can't.	We realize that our seed of suffering is active, and we do not hide or deny it. We allow ourselves to feel our emotions, but don't speak or act right away. When we've calmed down, we look at the present situation and decide how to act.

Acting from a place of suffering usually results in regret, misunderstanding, or harm. When we give ourselves the gift of stillness, we prevent our suffering from taking deeper root.

Instead of reacting, we can practice like this while walking slowly or sitting:

1. *Breathe in and acknowledge* that the seed of suffering has been activated in me.

2. *Breathe out and allow* all your bodily sensations to be exactly what they are. This will be unpleasant, but those feelings in you are in need of your acceptance and love.

3. *Breathe in and remind yourself* that perceptions are often clouded when suffering is strong.

4. *Breathe out and remember* your commitment to wait until your body is calm before acting or speaking.

By creating this space, we allow our nervous system to regulate itself. Our emotions might be quite intense, and that's okay. They won't last forever. When we no longer feel the immediate grip of suffering, we can look at our situation with greater clarity. Often, what seemed intolerable or urgent when suffering was strong appears much more manageable once we have calmed our body and mind.

SEEING CLEARLY AFTER THE STORM

Once the body returns to a state of relaxation, we can revisit the situation with fresh eyes. With suffering no longer distorting our vision, we may see possibilities that we could not have imagined before. We might recognize that someone's words were not as harsh as we initially thought, or that the difficulty we faced is not as overwhelming as it seemed. We can respond to life from a place of balance rather than reactivity.

Over time, it starts to feel easier and more natural to pause and breathe when you notice tension and agitation in your body. The more we return to the present moment, the less power the seed of suffering has to control our lives. Instead of strengthening suffering, we strengthen our capacity for mindfulness, patience, and compassion.

COMMUNICATING OUR NEEDS
WITH COMPASSION

When suffering is strong in us, it is easy to believe that others are responsible for our pain. We might think, "If only they acted differently, I wouldn't feel this way." This belief, though understandable, often leads to resentment and conflict. The peace treaty invites us to make sure we're seeing others clearly before responding to them.

One of the most powerful ways to do this is through *clear and compassionate communication*. When we recognize that the seed of suffering is strong in us, we can communicate this to those we love. We might say:

"The seed of suffering in me is strong right now. It doesn't take much to trigger it. I'm working to heal, and I need your support. Please try not to water this seed in me."

By sharing this openly, we help others understand our struggles without blame. This creates space for mutual understanding, allowing those around us to support our healing rather than unknowingly reinforcing our pain.

THE COMMITMENT TO PEACE

A true peace treaty is a unilateral commitment to mindfulness, compassionate communication, and self-awareness. It's a promise to nurture healing rather than reinforce suffering, even when other people are lost in their own pain.

By recognizing when suffering is present, choosing not to water its seeds, communicating with love, and returning to our breath, we transform not only our own experience but the world around us. We are building peace—one step, one breath, one mindful moment at a time.

The work of healing and transformation is lifelong, and each moment of awareness strengthens our capacity. The more we practice, the easier it becomes to recognize suffering without being caught by it. Over time, we develop a deeper resilience, and our relationships become rooted in understanding.

HOLDING
YOUR PAIN
ACCEPTANCE

One of the most radical and transformative practices in Buddhist psychology is the practice of holding our pain with loving-awareness. Instead of running away from suffering or trying to silence it, we invite it into our awareness with care and compassion. This is not a passive acceptance of suffering but an active process of embracing it, the way a loving parent holds a crying baby. When we bring our suffering into the presence of our mindfulness, something powerful happens: It begins to change.

WELCOMING THE SEED OF SUFFERING

Our emotions exist as seeds in the garden of our minds. Some seeds, like joy and gratitude, are easy to appreciate. Others, like fear, anger, or grief, are much harder. However, every human life contains both kinds of emotions. Unpleasant mental states will always arise, no matter how skillfully you might be living. If we don't know how to relate to them, we can create a lot of unnecessary suffering. When we get angry at our anger, or when we're afraid of our fear, those emotions just spiral. We need another way.

Holding your pain begins with an invitation. Instead of running from suffering, we allow it to arise. But we do not invite it alone—we also bring forth the seed of loving-awareness. This is the key. When suffering arises in isolation, it can be overwhelming. But when we bring mindfulness, gentleness, and curiosity to our suffering, it transforms.

THE POWER OF LOVING-AWARENESS

Loving-awareness is like a fragrant flower blooming in the garden of the mind. Its scent permeates everything it touches, including suffering. When the seed of suffering is strong, we do not need to fear it. Instead, we hold it with the warmth of our own awareness. This simple act of recognition—*I see you, suffering. I am here for you.*—can change the way we relate to our pain.

One way to understand this practice is to imagine your suffering as a crying baby. When a baby cries, we don't ignore them, scold them, or push them away. We pick them up, hold them close, and offer soothing care. We don't need to fix the problem immediately or make the crying stop; we simply hold the baby with love. In the same way, we can hold our suffering—not to get rid of it but to offer it the warmth and presence it needs to heal.

WORKING WITH THE
SENSATIONS OF SUFFERING

When suffering is present, we can focus on how it manifests as sensations in the body. Tension in the chest, tightness in the throat, heaviness in the stomach—these are some of the body's ways of expressing suffering. The first step in holding your pain is to become aware of these sensations.

Try This Practice

1. Find a quiet space and sit comfortably. Bring your awareness to your breath, allowing it to settle into a natural rhythm.

2. Notice any sensations in your body. Where do you feel tension, discomfort, or pain? If you notice only relaxation, you can deliberately invite suffering to manifest by thinking of something challenging (but not too painful while you're beginning).

3. Instead of resisting these sensations, bring a sense of kindness toward them. Place a gentle hand over the area, as if offering comfort to a dear friend.

4. Whisper to yourself, "I see you. I am here for you. In the present moment, you are safe and loved."

5. If the intensity of suffering is too strong, allow yourself to step back. Keep the intensity between a 3 and 7

out of 10. If it feels overwhelming, shift your focus to something beautiful or take a walk outside.

EXPERIMENTING WITH LOVING-AWARENESS

Each person has a different way of expressing love and care. Some may find comfort in placing a hand over their heart, and others might visualize light surrounding their pain. Some may find soothing words helpful—"It's okay. I am here with you."—and others might connect with their suffering without words. The key is to experiment and find what feels most effective for you.

THE GRADUAL TRANSFORMATION
OF SUFFERING

Holding pain with loving-awareness is not about making it disappear forever. After practicing for some time, you might notice that all you can find in your body is peace and relaxation. However, your suffering will always return. It's true that your seed of suffering can become smaller over time, but it won't disappear entirely. If you practice with something and it returns the next day, don't worry. You did nothing wrong.

As your practice deepens, you notice it becomes easier and easier to respond to suffering with care and compassion. Your heart opens, and you experience less and less unnecessary and self-inflicted pain.

Holding our pain with loving-awareness is one of the most powerful gifts we can give ourselves. It is an act of profound courage. Instead of running from suffering, we meet it with presence. Instead of rejecting our pain, we hold it gently, allowing it to transform in the warmth of awareness.

7

YOURSELF AS A 5-YEAR-OLD CHILD
TRANSFORMING

THE RINGS OF A TREE

If you imagine a 100-year-old tree, it's clear that the 50-year-old tree is concretely present inside it. You can count the rings and point to the 50- or the 20-year-old tree. The tree's past is never really gone.

This is also true about human beings in the sense that our past experiences are stored in the connections of the neural networks in our brains. For example, if a teacher shamed you when you were 8 years old, new connections were made in your brain at that time, because that's how our brains store information. If you are still affected by that experience in any way, it means that some of those connections are still present in your brain, like the rings in a tree. We carry all of our past selves within us in this way.

MEETING YOUR YOUNGER
SELVES WITH COMPASSION

Healing requires that we turn toward the pain from our past with kindness. Instead of seeing it as a burden to be erased, we can learn to approach our pain as younger parts of ourselves that are still waiting to be seen, held, and understood. This process is at the core of self-compassion and trauma integration.

One powerful practice is to *visualize your past selves* as younger versions of you still residing within. Find a quiet space, close your eyes, and imagine your 5-year-old self (or another significant age) standing before you. What do they look like? How do they feel? What are they trying to tell you? Imagine sitting beside them, offering warmth and safety. Say to them: "I see you. I know how hard it was. You are not alone anymore."

As you practice, pay attention to the sensations in your body. If you start to feel overwhelmed at all, stop the visualization and name some things in the room with you. You might want to move your body or return to a strengthening practice to regulate your emotions until you return to a state of feeling safe.

It's possible to expand this practice to other younger versions of yourself: the teenager who felt misunderstood, the young adult who faced rejection or loss. Acknowledge them, validate their experiences, and remind them that they are no longer alone. You, the person you are today, have the power to care for them in a way they might not have received before.

CHANGING THE NARRATIVE OF YOUR PAST

Neuroscience tells us that memory is not fixed. Every time we recall a memory, it becomes flexible, open to being reshaped before it is stored again. This process, known as *memory reconsolidation*, means that when we revisit painful moments while introducing warmth and compassion, we can change the emotional tone of how those experiences are stored in our brains.

Rather than viewing the past as a series of unchangeable tragedies, we can begin to relate to our history with a sense of tenderness. A childhood marked by loneliness does not have to remain a source of despair—it can become a testament to resilience, a reminder of the strength that carried you through. The pain of the past can be rewritten not as something that broke you but as something that strengthened your ability to hold compassion, both for yourself and for others.

PRACTICES FOR INTEGRATING
THE RINGS OF YOUR LIFE

1. Journaling as a dialogue with your past selves
   o Take a few minutes each day to write to a past version of yourself. You might begin with "Dear one, I see you. I remember when you . . . " Write with the intention of bringing warmth and understanding to your past experiences.
   o Allow your younger self to respond. What would they say? What do they need to hear? This can become a powerful ongoing practice of self-connection.

2. Meditation: embracing your inner tree
   o Sit comfortably and imagine yourself as a great tree. With each breath, visualize your past selves as rings inside of you.
   o As you breathe, send love and acceptance to each layer of yourself. Let your breath soften the wounds of the past, reminding each version of you that they are safe and held.

3. Loving-kindness (metta) for your past selves
   o Traditional loving-kindness meditation can be adapted to focus on your past selves. Repeat these phrases while holding an image of a younger you in your mind:
     ◎ May you be happy.
     ◎ May you be safe.
     ◎ May you be free from suffering.
     ◎ May you feel loved.

Each repetition reinforces a new way of relating to the past, replacing self-judgment with self-compassion.

THE STRENGTH OF A WHOLE TREE

A tree is not defined by a single year of its life. It is the sum of all its experiences. In the same way, we are not bound by our most painful moments. By integrating each part of our story with compassion, we become stronger and more whole.

The path of healing is not about erasing the past but about learning to hold it with love. The 5-year-old you, the 15-year-old you, the 25-year-old you—each of them still exists within you, and each moment of pain is in need of love. As you continue to grow, your task is not to forget them, but to embrace them, allowing them to become sources of wisdom.

Through this practice, healing unfolds—not as an instant transformation but as a steady, patient deepening of self-acceptance.

8

DEEPENING DIALOGUE WITH YOUR YOUNGER SELF
TRANSFORMING

Find a quiet space where you feel safe and undisturbed. Close your eyes and take a few slow, deep breaths. Now, bring to mind an image of yourself as a 5-year-old child (or another age that feels significant). Picture your small hands, the shape of your face, the look in your eyes. What were you feeling at that time? Is there a moment of sadness, fear, hurt, or loneliness that still lingers within you?

As you hold this image, gently invite a sense of warmth and care to arise in your body. Imagine yourself as you are now, older and wiser, standing beside this child. See yourself connecting with the child, offering kindness and comfort. You might say:

"I see you. I know how hard it was. I know you felt alone.
I am here now, and I will always be here for you."

You may want to visualize picking up your younger self, holding them in your arms, or simply placing a hand on their back. Feel what it's like to give them the love and reassurance they need.

Go slow and stop if you're feeling overwhelmed.

REWRITING THE EMOTIONAL NARRATIVE

Painful childhood memories are often stored as implicit memories: deep emotional imprints rather than clear recollections. When these memories arise in adulthood, they can trigger shame, fear, or self-judgment. However, by actively sending compassion to our younger selves, we can introduce a new emotional experience into those memories, shifting their impact.

Try this exercise:

1. Recall a specific childhood moment when you felt alone, afraid, or unworthy.

2. Instead of reliving the pain, imagine your current self stepping into that moment as an ally.

3. Picture yourself kneeling beside your younger self, offering warmth and safety.

4. Say to them: "You are lovable just as you are. You don't need to change anything to be worthy of love."

5. Hold this visualization as long as you need, breathing warmth and kindness into it.

THE ROLE OF A COMPASSIONATE FIGURE

If sending love to yourself feels difficult, you might instead imagine a deeply compassionate figure: a nurturing grandparent, a spiritual teacher, or even a loving presence that exists only in your imagination. Picture this figure sitting with your 5-year-old self, whispering words of comfort and acceptance. They might say:

"May you be happy. May you be safe.
May you feel deeply loved."

By bringing this loving presence into your past, you can change the way your brain stores and relates to old pain.

HEALING THROUGH DAILY PRACTICE

Transforming childhood wounds is not a one-time exercise but a practice to return to whenever needed. Some ways to integrate this into daily life include:

○ Placing a hand on your heart each morning, picturing your younger self, and silently saying, "May you be loved."

○ Writing a letter to your younger self, expressing all the care and reassurance they longed for.

○ Using a childhood photo as a reminder to speak to yourself with kindness.

Each time you engage in this practice, you strengthen the neural pathways of self-compassion, teaching your nervous system that it is safe to hold your pain with love. Through this, you become not only the recipient of compassion but also its source, offering your inner child a refuge that is always available.

THE PROMISE OF SELF-COMPASSION

By learning to send love to your 5-year-old self, you are engaging in one of the most radical acts of healing. You are proving that time does not have to be a barrier to love. The child within you is still there, still waiting to be seen, heard, and embraced. By offering them what they needed, you are not only healing the past—you are transforming the present.

9

THE DISCOURSE
ON HAPPINESS
SUTRA STUDY

At first glance, the Buddha's *Discourse on Happiness* (*Maṅgala Sutta*) can feel simple, even basic. It reads a lot like a list that anyone's grandmother might have taped to her fridge. However, that simplicity is deceptive. What's actually being offered here is a radical teaching: a blueprint for a good life that doesn't depend on anything dramatic, glamorous, or external. It's a map of the causes and conditions that reliably lead to peace and contentment.

From this perspective, the list can be used in two related ways. First, we begin by asking questions like "What kind of life do I want to build?" and "How can I build a life that is full of peace and contentment?" We reflect on these questions in light of the Buddha's teaching and decide how his list relates to our lives. Rather than interpreting the list as concrete rules to follow, we use it to examine our own priorities.

Second, we can think about how much of our day-to-day energy goes toward cultivating these conditions for happiness, and how much is spent on things that might not be as important. In Buddhism, we distinguish between wholesome and unwholesome joy. Wholesome joy is anything that creates happiness in the present, and contributes toward our long-term happiness. Unwholesome joy is anything that creates happiness or pleasure in the present, but contributes to suffering in the future. In this discourse, the Buddha is trying to encourage us to prioritize wholesome joys over unwholesome ones.

Here is my own synopsis of the discourse: A deva, or angelic being, comes down to Earth to ask the Buddha, "What are the greatest blessings that lead to a happy life?" The Buddha offers a list of the greatest blessings:

1. To live and interact with wise people instead of foolish ones.

2. To live in a good environment, having planted good seeds, and knowing you're on the right path.

3. To have a chance to learn and grow, to be skillful in your work, and speak lovingly.

4. To serve and support your family and have a job that brings you happiness.

5. To be honest and generous with friends, family, and neighbors.

6. To be free from addiction.

7. To be humble and content with a simple life, learning about the spiritual path whenever you can.

8. To be open to change, and to have spiritual mentors in your life.

9. To understand the deepest spiritual teachings and find liberation.

10. To live in the world with your heart open to but undisturbed by the world.

Most of these are pretty straightforward, but I'd like to comment on number 10. In Buddhism, the quality of compassion (*karuna*) is our capacity to respond to suffering with openness and love. It's different from our normal conception of compassion. Most of us believe that being undisturbed by the world is only possible by closing our hearts and not caring. We believe that if we care about the world, all of the suffering will make us angry or hopeless. However, as our compassion grows, we learn how to respond to suffering with love. We begin being able to hold our own suffering more skillfully, as well as the greater suffering of the world. That's what the Buddha is saying in the last blessing. As our compassion grows, eventually we're able to open our hearts and feel love rather than despair at the state of our world. This is not easy, and certainly not an expectation. It's more describing how beneficial it can be to grow our compassion.

Here's a last practice for you as you reflect on this discourse. You can take a few minutes to breathe and repeat these phrases to yourself:

○ May I remember what truly matters to me.

○ May I give energy to what brings peace.

○ May I grow a life that feels good to be in—one small step at a time.

10

BRINGING JOY INTO THE WORLD
COMPASSIONATE ACTION

Our suffering and our happiness are not just personal—they are collective. When we suffer, our pain affects those around us. When we cultivate joy, that joy ripples outward, influencing others in ways we may not even realize. Thich Nhat Hanh taught that our happiness is not separate from the happiness of others. This means that learning to nourish joy is not a selfish act—it is a gift to the world.

THE WISDOM OF THE BANANA LEAF

In 2005, while living in Plum Village, a student asked Thich Nhat Hanh about the meaning of life. In response, he shared a story about meditating in the jungle in Vietnam. He was sitting by a young banana tree, contemplating its leaves. The tree had just three leaves—one fully grown, broad and dark green; another still curled up; and a third, light green and tender, just beginning to unfurl.

He said that as he looked at the eldest leaf, he saw that it was fully enjoying its life as a banana leaf—soaking in the sun, receiving the rain, and radiating beauty and peacefulness. But in doing so, it was not abandoning the other leaves. By nourishing itself, it was also nourishing the younger leaves, the tree, and the entire jungle.

Thich Nhat Hanh explained that we are like this banana leaf. When we cultivate happiness, when we care for ourselves with love and presence, we are not just helping ourselves—we are supporting the well-being of everyone around us.

SPREADING JOY BY WATERING POSITIVE SEEDS

We have already explored how to cultivate joy within ourselves by watering the positive seeds in our consciousness. Now, we can take this further by sharing that joy with others.

Here are some ways we can bring joy into the world:

1. *Practice deep presence.* As you grow in your ability to be present with yourself, you will find that you can also bring the same presence to others. Simply being fully present with another person can be a profound gift. Whether it is listening deeply, smiling, or offering a kind word, presence has the power to bring peace to those around us.

2. *Share your joy.* When you experience something beautiful—a sunrise, a kind moment, a feeling of

peace—share it. Tell someone about it. Let them feel it with you.

3. *Acts of kindness.* Small, unexpected acts of kindness have a powerful effect. Holding the door, sending a thoughtful message, offering help—these gestures create ripples of joy. When you perform an act of kindness, you can silently wish happiness and freedom for the other person.

4. *Encourage others.* When someone is struggling, remind them of their goodness and their strength. Your words can water the positive seeds in them, just as others have done for you.

5. *Allow yourself to shine.* The banana leaf absorbs the sun fully, and in doing so, it nourishes everything around it. When you feel joy, let it be visible. Give others permission to do the same.

A REFLECTION: SPREADING JOY

Take a few deep breaths and reflect:

○ How has someone else's joy or kindness affected you in the past?

○ What small action could you take today to bring joy to another person?

○ How can you let yourself receive joy more fully?

In bringing joy to others, we reinforce our own happiness. In nourishing ourselves, we nourish the world. Just like the banana leaf, we do not have to choose between personal well-being and collective well-being—they are one and the same.

SECOND CYCLE

11

INFINITE CONDITIONS
STRENGTHENING

In every moment of life, there are infinite reasons to suffer and infinite reasons to be happy.

For example, if you were to take a few minutes right now to make a list of everything that you *could* be upset about, you'd never run out of ideas. If you were to take the same amount of time to list everything that you *could* be happy about, you would also find an endless supply. This is always true, even in the best or worst moments of life.

Since there are always infinite conditions that could cause happiness or suffering, our experience largely depends on where we focus our attention. The mind has a strong habit of seeking out what is wrong—what is missing, broken, or painful—because evolution has conditioned us to be alert to potential threats. However, this habit can lead us into patterns of chronic dissatisfaction, stress, and suffering. The good news is that we can train ourselves to recognize the conditions for joy that are always present alongside the conditions for suffering.

THE HABIT OF FOCUSING ON SUFFERING

Once we recognize that every moment of life will always contain infinite conditions for suffering—unmet goals, conflicts with others, uncertainties about the future—we begin to see the importance of how we direct our attention. If we spend most of our energy rehearsing these narratives, we'll end up overwhelmed and exhausted. If we must wait for all our problems to be gone before allowing ourselves to be happy, that moment will never arrive.

Acknowledging the existence of suffering does not mean that we must be consumed by it. Instead, we can hold space for suffering while also recognizing that it's never the whole picture. Even in difficult times, there are sources of nourishment available to us—acts of kindness, the sensation of our breath flowing in and out, the presence of a loved one, the warmth of sunlight on our skin.

TRAINING THE MIND TO RECOGNIZE JOY

Training ourselves to recognize positive conditions doesn't mean we're denying our suffering; it's about balance. Instead of being lost in thoughts of what's lacking, we can bring our attention to what's present. Just as we might habitually focus on stress, we can cultivate the habit of noticing beauty and joy.

One way to practice is by intentionally shifting our focus. When you realize that you're dwelling on problems, take a moment to list what is also going well. This could be something as simple as appreciating the ability to move your body, the taste of your morning tea, or a kind gesture from a friend. By doing this regularly, we begin to rewire our brains to notice moments of peace and contentment more naturally.

FINDING BEAUTY IN THE ORDINARY

Over time, we can improve our ability to recognize small, everyday joys: elements of life that might seem insignificant compared to the weight of our struggles. However, as we learn to be fully present with simple moments, they can become profound sources of happiness.

A useful practice is to pause periodically and ask yourself, "What is not wrong in this moment?" Often, the answer is far more than we expect. My teacher, Thich Nhat Hanh, used to encourage us to *enjoy our nontoothache*. When we have a toothache, it's so obvious that not having one would make us really happy. However, once the toothache goes away, we forget. We can train ourselves to recognize the absence of a toothache as a condition for happiness.

THE BALANCE BETWEEN SUFFERING AND JOY

The awareness that every moment contains infinite conditions for suffering or happiness allows us to be more intentional about when it makes sense to focus on our pain, and when we'd benefit more from focusing on joy. The more we strengthen our ability to see both, the more resilient we become.

When we acknowledge both suffering and joy, we engage with life from a place of wholeness. We are no longer waiting for conditions to be perfect before we allow ourselves to be happy. We recognize that happiness and suffering are like the waves of the ocean—always present, always shifting.

12

NOWHERE TO GO, NOTHING TO DO
STRENGTHENING

Everywhere we turn, we're inundated with messages urging us to strive for more and to chase after the next milestone. We often feel that reality in the present moment is unacceptable, so we live in a state of near- constant struggle. We seek to fix things and accomplish things, but no matter how much we achieve, happiness and peace remain out of reach. We don't know how to appreciate the beauty that's present right now, and end up burned out.

However, there's another way to live. We can learn to rest in the present moment, and to find beauty in things as they are. We can learn that it's possible to work toward making things better while deeply loving the world as it is, in this moment. In fact, the quality of deep, radical acceptance gives us energy to do more than we ever could've done when we were motivated by disliking our lives and the world. Any path toward change begins by recognizing that things *are how they are*. Any path toward peace includes the ability to let go of struggle.

Right now, in this very moment, you are here. This present

moment is complete in itself, not lacking anything. When we stop searching for something outside of now, we begin to uncover the richness that is already here.

RECOGNIZING STRUGGLE AS STRUGGLE

When we're in the state of striving and struggling, we are normally caught by our ideas. We're not aware that our bodily sensations are bodily sensations. We're not aware that our thoughts are thoughts. Instead, we've been swept up by our feelings and thoughts, and carried away.

Try this:

O Ask yourself, "Do I feel able to fully accept the world as it is, in this moment?"

O If so, just enjoy that experience of radical acceptance.

O If not, don't try to force yourself to stop striving and struggling. Instead, notice that *your nonacceptance is part of the world as it is*, right now. The world is exactly as it is, and I feel a strong aversion to that world. That's how it is right now.

O Practice noticing that this is what's happening, and just allow it to be this way.

O Notice that your aversion is made of some bodily sensations (like tension) and some thoughts. Those bodily sensations and thoughts are part of the world as it is.

○ With each breath, allow your thoughts and bodily sensations to come and go, however they want to. Let your aversion stay or go. Just be willing to feel it. Notice how you feel after a few minutes.

This practice helps you learn how to accept your nonacceptance, instead of fighting with it.

RELEASING THE NEED TO STRUGGLE

Many of us have been conditioned to believe that if we aren't pushing ourselves, we are falling behind. This way of thinking keeps us locked in a cycle of striving, always anticipating what comes next rather than appreciating what is. But what if, instead of resisting the present, we allowed ourselves to settle into it? What if we considered the idea that this moment, as it is, holds everything we need—that there are already infinite conditions for happiness?

This doesn't mean giving up on our aspirations or ignoring our responsibilities. Rather, it's about balancing action with presence—recognizing that while we may work toward change, we can also find peace in the here and now. There is a deep sense of rest that comes from acknowledging that we do not need to fix or control everything in order to be okay.

DISCOVERING FREEDOM IN STILLNESS

Master Linji, a revered Zen master in the Tang dynasty in China and the founder of my lineage, introduced the idea of the "businessless person." It means someone who has let go of striving and instead moves through life with ease. This person isn't passive or disengaged. It's that they are no longer caught in the illusion that they must constantly chase something outside themselves. He described this way of being as *being without business* or *without busy-ness*. According to Linji, a businessless person might be great at business, in the sense that they might accomplish great things. However, they would never feel busy or pressured. Can you imagine living like that? It is the kind of person who knows that the world is already beautiful just the way it is. They act from a place of freedom and creativity rather than stress.

To embody this teaching is to stop measuring our worth by external achievements. It is to understand that the present moment is not an obstacle to be overcome but an experience to be lived fully. When we don't need to go anywhere or do anything special to be whole, we begin to feel a profound sense of belonging to life itself.

MORE PRACTICES FOR RESTING
IN THE PRESENT

Paradoxically, cultivating this sense of ease takes effort, especially in a culture that equates stillness with stagnation. Here are some simple ways to step into the experience of "nowhere to go, nothing to do."

1. Grounding Through Awareness

Take a moment to notice what is happening around you. The texture of the air, the sounds in the distance, the feeling of your body resting in space. There is no need to analyze or judge—simply observe. Let your awareness settle on what is, rather than what should be.

2. Sensing the Flow of Breath

The breath is always with us, a steady companion that requires no effort. Notice its natural rhythm. Feel the way it enters and leaves your body. Rather than trying to control it, allow yourself to be carried by its gentle flow, like a boat floating on calm waters.

3. Allowing Thoughts to Pass

The mind will wander—that is its nature. Many of our thoughts are about aspects of life that we want to change, or things that we believe we need for happiness to be possible. Instead of becoming frustrated when these thoughts arise, practice seeing them like clouds drifting across the sky. They come and go, but they don't define the sky itself. Your awareness remains spacious, untouched by passing mental activity.

4. Appreciating Simple Moments

Try to recognize that you already have enough conditions for happiness in this present moment—the warmth of the sun, the taste of a meal, the parts of your body that aren't in pain. These moments are not distractions from life; they are life. As you move through your day, try immersing yourself in them to cultivate gratitude and connection to the world around you.

THE ART OF LETTING LIFE BE

When we stop insisting that things must be different, we open ourselves to the beauty of what is. This doesn't mean that we cease to grow or evolve, but that we no longer base our happiness on what hasn't yet arrived.

Linji's teachings remind us that the most awakened state is one of simplicity—being fully ourselves, without the need for embellishment. The greatest wisdom is not in acquiring more knowledge or reaching new heights but in knowing that we already have everything we need.

There is deep freedom in realizing that we don't need to be anywhere other than where we are. In fact, it's impossible to be. When we release the urge to chase something just beyond reach, we find that life is already complete. This moment is enough. You are enough. And in that understanding, there is peace.

PRACTICING
SELF-COMPASSION
STRENGTHENING

Self-compassion is the foundation of emotional healing. It is the practice of extending the same kindness, patience, and understanding to ourselves that we would offer to a dear friend. When we experience suffering, pain, or failure, our habitual reaction is often to judge ourselves harshly. However, through mindful self-compassion, we can learn to meet our pain with warmth and care rather than criticism.

WHY SELF-COMPASSION MATTERS

Many of us carry deeply ingrained beliefs that we must be hard on ourselves in order to succeed or improve. We might believe that self-judgment keeps us motivated or prevents us from making mistakes. However, research and our own experience both show us that self-criticism normally leads to more stress, anxiety, and emotional suffering. When we approach ourselves with compassion instead of judgment, we create a supportive inner environment where healing and growth can naturally unfold.

By sending compassion to ourselves, we learn to shift from a mindset of self-criticism to one of self-care. This shift not only reduces our suffering but also strengthens our ability to be present for others. Self-compassion is not selfish. Instead, it replenishes our emotional reserves so that we can extend care and kindness more freely to those around us.

THE NEAR ENEMIES OF SELF-COMPASSION

In Buddhist psychology, a near enemy is something that looks similar to a virtue but is actually a distortion of it. In order to grow our self-compassion, it's important to recognize the difference between the quality that we truly want to develop and its near enemies.

SELF-INDULGENCE VS. SELF-COMPASSION

One of the most common misconceptions about self-compassion is that it means giving ourselves unlimited permission to do whatever we want, without regard for consequences. This is *self-indulgence*, not self-compassion. Self-compassion involves recognizing our suffering and responding with kindness while still holding on to our deepest aspirations. True self-compassion is not about avoiding effort or accountability—it is about supporting ourselves with understanding as we work toward meaningful goals.

If we mistakenly believe that self-compassion means allowing ourselves to avoid challenges or difficult emotions, we may end up reinforcing patterns of avoidance that ultimately lead to greater suffering. Genuine self-compassion acknowledges our pain but also calls us toward wisdom and action.

SELF-PITY VS. SELF-COMPASSION

Self-pity is another near enemy of self-compassion. While both involve recognizing suffering, self-pity can keep us stuck in a cycle of feeling powerless and overwhelmed. When we pity ourselves, we become absorbed in our own distress without seeking ways to care for ourselves. Self-compassion, on the other hand, acknowledges pain but also fosters a sense of agency—we recognize that suffering is a universal experience and that we have the capacity to meet it with warmth and care.

A key distinction between self-pity and self-compassion is that self-compassion broadens our perspective. It helps us see that we are not alone in our struggles and encourages us to take steps toward healing. Self-pity, by contrast, isolates us, making it harder to connect with others and to see the possibilities for change.

PASSIVITY VS. SELF-COMPASSION

Compassion is inherently active. If we see someone in pain, we don't simply acknowledge their suffering—we take action to help whenever possible. The same principle applies to self-compassion. If we mistake self-compassion for passivity, we can end up failing to make changes that would genuinely improve our well-being.

For example, if we are in an unhealthy relationship or a toxic work environment, self-compassion does not mean simply accepting the situation and resigning ourselves to continued suffering. It means recognizing our pain, treating ourselves with kindness, and taking thoughtful steps to care for ourselves, whether that means setting boundaries, seeking support, or making a change.

EGOTISM VS. SELF-COMPASSION

True self-compassion is inclusive—it values our well-being without diminishing the well-being of others. However, a near enemy of self-compassion is egotism, where self-care becomes an excuse for self-importance or entitlement. When self-compassion is misinterpreted as a justification for prioritizing our needs at the expense of others, it isolates us and undermines our healing.

Real self-compassion enhances our capacity for connection and empathy. It doesn't mean seeing ourselves as more deserving than others but rather as equally deserving of care and kindness. Practicing self-compassion helps us cultivate a greater sense of balance— honoring our own needs while also remaining attuned to the needs of those around us.

RECOGNIZING THE NEAR ENEMIES
IN OUR OWN PRACTICE

When we're first learning to practice self-compassion, it's normal to find ourselves practicing a near enemy instead. However, if we notice ourselves becoming self-indulgent, wallowing in self-pity, avoiding necessary action, or using self-compassion as a shield for egotism, we can gently guide ourselves back to the heart of true self-compassion.

A simple way to check whether our self-compassion practice is genuine is to ask:

O "Is my practice actually helping me grow and heal?"

O "Am I balancing awareness of my suffering with gratitude for what is beautiful in my life?"

O "Is my practice strengthening my connection with others or making me more isolated?"

When we approach self-compassion with clarity, we can harness its full potential as a source of healing, resilience, and genuine self-care. Understanding its near enemies allows us to deepen our practice and ensure that we're truly fostering kindness toward ourselves in a way that leads to growth and transformation.

METHODS OF SENDING COMPASSION TO YOURSELF

There are many ways to practice self-compassion. You will find some are much easier or much more difficult for you. Over many years of teaching these practices, I've come to learn that there's no way to know which practice will be the easiest for a specific person other than trying them. At the beginning, we're looking for the easiest way for you to connect with the healing energy of self-compassion. Below are a few techniques to experiment with.

1. Placing a Hand Over Your Heart

Try placing a gentle hand over your heart. This physical gesture sends a signal to your nervous system that you are safe and cared for. This practice can be particularly helpful when you feel overwhelmed or emotionally distressed:

○ Find a quiet space and take a few slow, deep breaths.

○ Place one or both hands over your heart, applying gentle pressure.

○ As you breathe in, imagine drawing in warmth and kindness. As you breathe out, release any tension or self-judgment.

○ You may silently say to yourself, "May I be kind to myself in this moment. May I give myself the care I need."

2. Using Self-Compassionate Phrases

For some of us, words are powerful. You can change these phrases to be personal and meaningful to you. Some examples include:

○ "May I be happy. May I be safe. May I be free from suffering."

○ "I am doing my best, and that is enough."

○ "I choose to be kind to myself in this moment."

You can say these phrases aloud, or repeat them silently in your mind. Over time, these words can become a natural source of comfort and reassurance.

3. Visualizing Compassion Toward Yourself
Visualization can be a powerful tool for cultivating self-compassion.

○ Close your eyes and take a few deep breaths.

○ Picture yourself as you were when you were a child. Imagine looking into the eyes of your younger self.

○ Extend warmth and kindness to this child. Imagine wrapping them in a loving embrace or whispering words of reassurance.

○ If it feels right, say to your younger self, "You are loved. You are worthy. You deserve kindness."

○ Slowly bring your awareness back to the present moment, carrying the feeling of compassion with you.

This practice helps cultivate a sense of self-acceptance and care, particularly for past wounds that may still influence our present experiences.

4. Practicing Self-Compassion in Difficult Moments
Painful emotions will always be a part of life. Learning to meet them with self-compassion is a key skill for healing. The next time you feel frustration, sadness, or fear, try the following steps:

1. *Pause and acknowledge.* Notice the emotion without judgment. Simply recognize that you are struggling.

2. *Validate your feelings.* Remind yourself that suffering is a natural part of life. You are not alone in your pain.

3. *Offer yourself comfort.* Use a compassionate phrase, a hand over your heart, or deep breathing to bring warmth and kindness into the moment.

By practicing self-compassion in difficult times, we create a habit of responding to ourselves with care rather than self-criticism.

BRINGING SELF-COMPASSION INTO DAILY LIFE

Integrating self-compassion into everyday life doesn't require grand gestures—it's about small, consistent acts of kindness toward yourself. Here are a few ways to make it part of your routine:

○ Start each morning with a few self-compassionate phrases.

○ Take pauses throughout the day to check in with your emotions and see if there's a part of you that needs love.

○ Keep a journal where you write messages of kindness to yourself.

○ Set a reminder on your phone to pause during the day, take a deep breath and offer yourself a moment of compassion.

If you can find a practice that feels natural to you, use it as often as you can. Over time, responding to suffering with love can become a habit.

14

SUFFERING IS THE ABSENCE OF LOVE
ACCEPTANCE

At the core of every form of suffering—anger, fear, and grief—is the absence of love. When we suffer, it is because something in us perceives a disconnection from warmth, safety, and belonging. Using Buddhist psychology, we can examine suffering through the lens of craving, aversion, and love. When craving and aversion dominate our experience, love is absent. If we want to transform suffering, we must learn to recognize the role of love in healing our pain.

CRAVING, AVERSION, AND THE ABSENCE OF LOVE

Craving and aversion always arise together. Whenever we look at the world and wish it were different, craving and aversion are present. If we crave comfort, we simultaneously feel aversion toward discomfort. If we're feeling aversion toward someone's anger, then we're also craving freedom or escape from that anger. These forces shape our perception of reality, and are the most foundational elements that give rise to the experience of dissatisfaction.

On the other hand, love dissolves the illusion that things must be different for us to be happy. When we look at something and see past our mental projections, we can experience the thing in itself. When that happens we can see its sacredness and beauty. Without the belief that it *should* be different, we can recognize its inherent worth. This is love—not in the sentimental sense but as an openness to reality as it is. When we truly love ourselves or another person, we are not grasping after strengths and disgusted by weaknesses. We are seeing the whole, and saying *yes*.

SUFFERING AS A FUNCTION OF THE THREAT-RESPONSE SYSTEM

Human suffering is deeply tied to our threat-response system. The body and mind are constantly scanning for potential threats, whether they are real or imagined. When we identify something as a danger, we mobilize to confront it, avoid it, or seek help. Embedded in this process is aversion—the rejection of what we perceive as harmful.

Craving and aversion exist in every moment of suffering. Fear arises because we crave safety. Anger arises because we crave justice. Grief arises because we have aversion to loss. This cycle is self-perpetuating—our suffering feeds our craving and aversion, which in turn strengthens our suffering.

BREAKING THE CYCLE:
LOVING OUR CRAVING AND AVERSION

Once we see how craving and aversion fuel our suffering, we might be tempted to push them away. We might feel aversion toward our aversion, and crave a life free from craving. But this only continues the cycle. The way out is not to reject craving and aversion but to meet them with love.

Craving is not inherently bad—it is simply a part of us trying to secure happiness. Aversion is not a flaw—it is the mind's way of seeking safety. If we can look at these aspects of ourselves and see their beauty, we will no longer be caught by them. Craving and aversion will arise, but we will not be consumed by them. Instead, we can remain rooted in love.

PRACTICING LOVE IN THE
FACE OF SUFFERING

The practice of love is not about forcing ourselves to feel a certain way. It is about shifting how we relate to our suffering. Instead of seeing pain as an enemy, we hold it with the warmth of loving-awareness. We acknowledge our craving and aversion, not as obstacles but as parts of us that are seeking care.

A Simple Practice

1. *Recognize when suffering arises.* Notice when you feel anger, fear, or grief. Identify the energies of craving and aversion at play.

2. *Invite loving-awareness.* Instead of rejecting what you feel, breathe deeply and say to yourself, "This too is worthy of love."

3. *Hold your suffering like a crying baby.* Imagine holding a baby who is upset—not needing to silence them but simply offering warmth and presence.

4. *Stay present with love.* As the energy of craving and aversion move through you, stay rooted in love. Let it permeate the experience, softening the edges of suffering.

FREEDOM THROUGH LOVE

When we meet suffering with love, we break free from its grip. We no longer have to believe that things must be different for us to be happy. We no longer have to run from our pain or try to fix it immediately. Love does not eliminate suffering but it transforms our relationship to it. In this space of radical acceptance we find peace, and with peace, we find freedom.

15

TRANSFORMATION
AND THE BRAIN
TRANSFORMING

One of the most significant insights of modern neuroscience is that memory is not fixed. Contrary to what many of us assume, our memories aren't stored like paper files in a cabinet—rather, each time we recall a memory, it becomes temporarily malleable before being rewritten in our brain. This happens because the core function of our memories is not to keep an accurate record of our lives. It is to learn from our experiences so we can interpret the present in a way that makes it predictable. Therefore, when a memory becomes active, the brain wants to update it with any relevant new information.

This process, known as memory reconsolidation, is central to the process of healing from trauma. When we bring a painful memory into consciousness while simultaneously experiencing self-compassion, we can fundamentally alter our relationship to the past. Buddhist practice and self-compassion training provide us with the tools to guide this transformation.

THE SCIENCE OF MEMORY RECONSOLIDATION

Neuroscientist Joseph LeDoux and his colleagues have extensively studied memory reconsolidation, showing that when a memory is recalled, it temporarily enters a labile state before it is stored again. During this window, the memory is not only open to modification but can also integrate new emotional and cognitive perspectives. This means that if we can bring up a traumatic memory while simultaneously activating the brain's care circuits—through practices like self-compassion, loving-kindness, or mindfulness—we can reshape the emotional associations tied to that memory.

It is likely this neurological process that makes healing trauma possible. Trauma is often stored as implicit memory, in body-based sensations and deep emotional imprints that can be triggered without conscious awareness. When these implicit memories arise, they often evoke the same distressing emotions and physiological responses that were present during the original event. However, it's possible to disrupt this cycle, and offer the nervous system a new, more compassionate experience in response to the memory.

HOW MEMORY RECONSOLIDATION
ALIGNS WITH BUDDHIST PRACTICE

Buddhist psychology has long recognized the impermanent and constructed nature of our experience, including our memories and self-narratives. The teachings on *anicca* (impermanence) remind us that nothing is fixed—not even our past. While we cannot change what happened, we can change the way we hold and relate to it. This is where the practice of self-compassion becomes essential.

My teacher, Thich Nhat Hanh, often taught that the seeds of suffering that were strengthened in the past don't have to bear fruit in the present. He emphasized that mindfulness and compassion can transform suffering by holding it with love rather than resistance. When we recall a painful memory and meet it with compassion instead of fear or avoidance, we create the conditions for healing. Instead of being imprisoned by our past, we can reshape our inner world to reflect kindness, understanding, and resilience.

A PRACTICE FOR HEALING TRAUMA THROUGH MEMORY RECONSOLIDATION

Here's one structured way to work with memory reconsolidation. You can experiment to find a process that works for you. The vital element is activating a painful memory while introducing the energy of compassion.

1. *Find a safe space.* Choose a quiet place where you feel comfortable and secure. Sit in a relaxed but upright posture, allowing your body to be at ease.

2. *Ground yourself in the present.* Before bringing up a painful memory, anchor yourself in the present moment. Feel your breath moving in and out, sense your body in space, and notice any points of contact with the floor or chair.

3. *Bring up a difficult memory gently.* Choose a memory that carries some emotional weight but is not overwhelming. Visualize the event with as much or as little detail as feels safe. Notice any bodily sensations that arise.

4. *Introduce compassion.* Imagine sending compassion to your past self. You might place a hand on your heart and silently say, "I see your suffering. You were doing the best you could. I am here for you now." Or you might imagine an older, wiser version of yourself offering kindness and understanding to the part of you that experienced this pain. Change the words to make them appropriate for you.

5. *Reframe the narrative.* Instead of seeing the memory through the lens of shame or fear, view it with a sense of growth and resilience. Ask yourself, "If I were always lovable and deserved good things, how could I explain why this happened?"

6. *Return to the present with gratitude.* After spending a few minutes with the memory, bring your awareness back to the present. Acknowledge the courage it takes to face the past with compassion. Feel gratitude for your strength and capacity for healing.

OVERCOMING BARRIERS TO TRANSFORMATION

Many people struggle with working directly with traumatic memories due to their intensity. If a memory feels too overwhelming, it may be necessary to first build a foundation of emotional regulation through mindfulness and self-compassion practices. The more we strengthen the brain's care circuits, the more resilience we develop in facing our pain.

Additionally, it is crucial to recognize that healing is not about erasing the past but about changing our relationship to it. Some memories will always carry sadness, but by holding them with warmth rather than resistance, they lose their ability to dominate our present experience.

THE PROMISE OF TRANSFORMATION

Memory reconsolidation and transformation offer a profound promise: that we are not permanently defined by what has happened to us. Buddhist practice reminds us that suffering is not personal—it is universal—and that by transforming our pain, we contribute to a collective healing that extends beyond ourselves.

Every time we choose to meet a painful memory with kindness, we weaken the hold of fear and suffering in our lives. Through deliberate practice, we can replace old patterns of self-judgment with care, and turn wounds into sources of wisdom and resilience. This is the path of healing: not through force or suppression but through the gentle, persistent power of compassion.

16

TAKING REFUGE
IN ONESELF
SUTRA STUDY

The *Discourse on Taking Refuge in Oneself* teaches that true safety and refuge can only be found within ourselves. This teaching is especially important in healing trauma, as trauma often leaves us feeling unmoored, seeking safety outside of ourselves, or disconnected from our inner strength. Learning to take refuge in ourselves means discovering that stability, safety, and healing are possible within our own awareness and presence.

In the discourse itself, the Buddha talks about the deaths of two of his most senior students. He warns all of his disciples against the belief that anyone or anything outside of themselves could liberate them. Instead, he points each student to look within at their own capacity for healing and freedom.

THE THREE JEWELS WITHIN

In Buddhist tradition, taking refuge often means turning toward the Three Jewels: the Buddha (awakening), the Dharma (the path), and the Sangha (the community). This discourse, however, reminds us that these refuges are also found within. For trauma survivors, this means that we do not have to wait for external validation or ideal conditions to heal—we already have everything we need inside us.

○ *Taking refuge in the Buddha within* means trusting in our own capacity for wisdom and transformation. Trauma can make us feel broken or unworthy, but we can remember: "I have the capacity to wake up. Healing is possible for me."

○ *Taking refuge in the Dharma within* means recognizing that the teachings of healing and liberation are not just concepts but lived experiences. Each moment of mindfulness, each breath taken with awareness, is a direct expression of the path.

○ *Taking refuge in the Sangha within* reminds us that we are never truly alone. Even when external support feels distant, we can call upon the parts of ourselves that hold kindness, wisdom, and care. We carry the presence of those who have helped us, and we can become our own source of loving support.

COMING HOME TO THE PRESENT MOMENT

This discourse teaches that the deepest refuge can be found in the present moment. While trauma might pull us into the past or fill us with fear about the future, anchoring in the present—through awareness of breath, body, or feelings—can create a safe space within ourselves.

A simple practice for this is:

○ Breathing in, I come home to myself.

○ Breathing out, I take refuge in this moment.

This reminds us that, no matter what has happened before, this moment is fresh and full of possibility. Each breath can be a return to safety and self-compassion.

REBUILDING TRUST IN OURSELVES

One of the deepest wounds of trauma is often a loss of trust—trust in others, in the world, and in ourselves. Taking refuge in oneself is an act of reclaiming that trust. This does not mean forcing ourselves to feel safe immediately but rather, cultivating small moments of self-trust.

○ Noticing when we are kind to ourselves.

○ Honoring our instincts when we need rest or space.

○ Recognizing moments of inner strength, even if they feel small.

Through mindfulness and self-compassion, we slowly rebuild a sense of inner refuge. We come to see that while the world is unpredictable, there is a place within us that can always offer stability and care.

HEALING AS A RETURN TO OURSELVES

The path of healing is not about becoming someone new—it is about returning to the wholeness that has always been there. Taking refuge in oneself means seeing that, despite suffering, we still carry the seeds of peace, wisdom, and love. The more we nurture these qualities, the more they become a sanctuary within us.

Through this practice, we learn that refuge is not a place we must search for—it is a presence we cultivate. In every mindful breath, in every moment of kindness toward ourselves, we take refuge.

17

RIGHT VIEW
SUTRA STUDY

In Buddhism, Right View means a way of seeing the world with perfect clarity and understanding. The underlying purpose of every Buddhist philosophy and practice is to give you the direct experience of seeing the world through the lens of Right View. It is also the first step on the *Noble Eightfold Path*.

When we suffer, our first reaction is often to personalize it: Why is this happening to me? What did I do wrong? But Right View reminds us that suffering is never just personal. It arises from many factors—our transmissions from our parents, past generations, and the conditions of the world around us. By understanding this, we loosen the grip of self-blame and shift toward wisdom and compassion.

Right View also helps us see that nothing is permanent. Our suffering, like everything else, is in constant motion. No matter how deep our pain feels in the present moment, it is not fixed. Understanding *impermanence (anicca)* allows us to hold suffering with more spaciousness, knowing that it, too, will change.

Additionally, Right View includes the teaching of *non-self (anatta)*. Trauma often makes us feel defined by our suffering, as if our pain is who we are. But Buddhism teaches that the self is not a solid, unchanging entity—it is a flowing, interconnected process. We are more than our suffering, more than our past, more than the stories we have told ourselves. This insight is liberating because it means we are not trapped in old identities. We can grow, change, and redefine ourselves.

Thich Nhat Hanh taught that if mindfulness is not informed by the wisdom of Right View, it can actually reinforce harmful patterns. For example, if our practice is built on individualism or materialism, it does not liberate us. But when we see our suffering in its full context, we develop compassion instead of blame. We stop seeing pain as a sign of personal failure and begin to understand it as part of the human condition. This shift is essential for healing.

Right View helps us understand that we are not separate from the causes of our suffering. And because suffering has causes, it also has conditions that allow it to transform. We are not trapped. With practice, we can change our relationship to pain and cultivate freedom.

INTERBEING: NOTHING EXISTS ALONE

Interbeing (*paāicca-samuppāda*) is one of the most fundamental parts of Right View. It means that nothing exists independently—everything is connected. Thich Nhat Hanh often used a piece of paper to illustrate this teaching. We all know that paper is made from a tree. However, most of us would say that after paper has been made, the tree no longer exists. If we look more deeply, we can see the tree is still present in the piece of paper. Imagine removing the tree from the paper. What would exist? We can see that the tree isn't really gone. It has transformed into paper. Looking even more deeply, we see that the sunshine, the rain, and the labor of the person who made the paper are all still present in the paper. If you try to remove any of them, then the paper can't exist. Therefore, we say that the paper is made out of many *nonpaper elements*, such as a tree, the sun, and the rain. Those nonpaper elements are present in the paper, and if you removed them, the paper couldn't exist. Going a little further, we say that the paper cannot "be" on its own. It must "inter-be" with all of these nonpaper elements. This is true for you, me, and the whole world. We are made of *non-self elements*, and we "inter-are" with all of them.

This teaching is vital to the process of healing. Trauma isolates us. It makes us believe that our suffering is ours alone. But interbeing shows us that our pain is woven into a larger fabric: our ancestors, our culture, our relationships. This doesn't mean we dismiss our suffering—rather, it allows us to hold it with greater understanding. We see that healing ourselves is also a way of healing the world.

When we understand interbeing, we stop thinking of self-compassion and compassion for others as separate things. If everything is interconnected, then the care we give ourselves ripples outward. By tending to our own suffering, we create the conditions for more peace in the world around us.

HEALING THROUGH RIGHT
VIEW AND INTERBEING

How do we apply these teachings in practice?

○ *Recognizing shared suffering.* When we feel overwhelmed, we can remind ourselves: This pain is not mine alone. All pain is collective and shared. This shifts our experience from isolation to connection.

○ *Tracing the roots of our pain.* Instead of personalizing suffering, we can look deeply: Where did this pain come from? How was it transmitted to me? This helps loosen shame and self-blame.

○ *Seeing healing as part of a greater whole.* When we heal, we do not heal just for ourselves. Our healing impacts our relationships, our communities, and even future generations. Healing is an act of interbeing.

By practicing Right View and interbeing, we see that we are not alone. Our suffering is not separate from the world, and our healing is not separate either. We do not have to carry the weight of our pain in isolation. Instead, we learn to hold it with wisdom, knowing that transformation is always possible.

18

EMPOWERMENT
THROUGH SERVICE
COMPASSIONATE ACTION

We're aware that in every moment of life, we can turn toward what is beautiful in order to be nourished by it. We can turn toward what is painful in order to embrace it with love and heal. At the same time, we can also choose to turn toward opportunities to support others. In doing so, we step out of the part of ourselves that holds our pain, and into the part that is capable and full of agency. Finding a balance between all of these different aspects of reality is how we keep our practice strong.

In Buddhism, there are many stories about service and generosity as the fruits of understanding: people like Visakha, the Great Laywoman, whose granddaughter died and it nearly broke her heart. When the Buddha helped her see that her grief was made out of deep love, and that everyone she knows will die someday, she dedicated herself entirely to serving others. However, it is also true that service can heal the one who serves.

HOW SERVICE HEALS

In both research and contemplative experience, acts of service support healing in several key ways:

○ *Reducing isolation.* Serving others—especially in gentle, low-stakes ways—draws us back into relationship. We feel part of something again.

○ *Restoring agency.* When we're able to give to another person or animal and they benefit from what we do, we often get to experience the joy of receiving gratitude. This is a performance. It's the feedback that our efforts to make the other person's life better had their intended effect.

○ *Cultivating joy.* The Brahmaviharas—loving-kindness, compassion, sympathetic joy, and equanimity—are qualities we strengthen through action. Practicing service waters the seeds of these states in our minds and bodies.

○ *Balancing attention.* Suffering can consume our awareness. Helping others redirects our focus—not as distraction but as rebalancing. We're reminded that the world is vast, and that it needs us.

GENTLE WAYS TO BEGIN

If you're early in your healing journey, the idea of service might feel overwhelming. That's okay. Don't aim for anything grand. Aim for some small act that could benefit a living being.

Try one of these:

○ Offer water to a plant or food to a bird.

○ Send a message to someone you know is struggling.

○ Pick up trash during a walk and offer the act to the Earth.

○ Volunteer for something that feels meaningful.

○ Cook something for a neighbor, even if you don't deliver it yet.

○ Sit with a shelter animal, or quietly send compassion to people in a waiting room.

The key is that it feels sustainable. You're not saving the world all at once. You're remembering that you're a part of it.

A PRACTICE: "MAY MY HEALING SERVE"

Before a small act of kindness, try this reflection:

Breathing in, I remember my own suffering.

Breathing out, I remember the suffering of others.

Breathing in, I touch my capacity to heal.

Breathing out, I offer that healing to the world.

This isn't self-sacrifice. It's alignment. You are bringing the fruits of your practice into the stream of life. As Thich Nhat Hanh once said, "The way out is in. But the way forward is also through love in action."

THIRD CYCLE

19

THE JOY OF LETTING GO
STRENGTHENING

Thich Nhat Hanh used to say, "If you know what happiness looks like, you'll never be happy." By this, he meant that our ideas about happiness can become an obstacle. If we believe that we will only be happy when we achieve a certain goal—when we find the right relationship, reach a milestone in our career, or fix a particular pattern in our life—we're creating an image of happiness that exists only in our minds. This image is not reality. It may help orient us toward meaningful goals, but it also has unintended consequences.

The thought "I will be happy when I achieve this" implies that happiness isn't possible until reality matches our idea. This is one of the most fundamental misunderstandings we can have. Reality itself will never perfectly conform to our expectations. Reality is sacred because it's exactly what it is, not because it aligns with the stories we tell ourselves about how things should be. If we hold tightly to our ideas about happiness, we can spend our lives chasing a mirage, always waiting for some imagined future to bring us peace.

LETTING GO OF THE IDEA OF HAPPINESS

The practice of letting go is about learning to appreciate reality as it is, rather than how we think it should be. This doesn't mean that we give up our aspirations or stop striving for meaningful change. Rather, it means that we stop postponing happiness. We learn to recognize that peace and joy are possible right now, in this very moment. There are already infinite conditions for happiness if we remember to look for them.

We can practice this by coming home to our breathing and the sensations in our body. If we can sit quietly, even for a few moments, and experience a moment with no thoughts—just the breath, just the body—we can begin to glimpse the reality beyond our mental projections. What does the world feel like when there is no thought telling us how it *should* be? In these moments of quiet, we touch something real and vast, something that is not bound by our expectations.

Alternatively, we can relate to our thinking like it's a well-meaning friend who is constantly giving unsolicited advice: "You'd be happier like this. You should really do that. You don't want this in your life." Like any friend's advice, some of it might be good, and some of it will be off the mark. Either way, it's just advice, and we don't need to believe it. Relating to your thoughts in this way can help you not take them too seriously, while also not resenting how insistent they are.

FREEDOM THROUGH LETTING GO

Many of us hold on to our ideas about happiness because we are afraid. We fear that if we let go of our expectations, we will become aimless and passive. But the truth is the opposite. Letting go is an act of courage. It allows us to meet life with openness and curiosity rather than rigid demands.

Thich Nhat Hanh used to tell a story about a farmer who had lost his cows. The Buddha was sitting with his monks and enjoying their meal in the forest when a farmer came running down the path. The farmer shouted, "Have you monks seen my cows? They are all I have in the world and they've run away. If I can't find them, I will kill myself."

With compassion, the Buddha said to the farmer, "I'm sorry but your cows have not come this way. You should look in the other direction." The farmer ran off, and the Buddha turned back to his monks. After a silence, he said, "How fortunate we are that we have no cows to lose." The Buddha and his monks owned nothing but a bowl for begging and their robes. The moral of the story is that when we cling tightly to our attachments—whether they are material possessions, relationships, or ideas—we create suffering for ourselves. We fear loss, and in that fear, we become trapped. But when we release our grip, we find a deep, unexpected relief.

After telling this story, Thich Nhat Hanh would ask us, "What are the cows you're holding on to? What do you believe is absolutely necessary for your happiness? What would happen if you let go of your cows?" He didn't mean deliberately pushing away precious things, but just loosening our grip on them.

PRACTICES FOR LETTING GO

Letting go is not something we do once—it is a practice, something we return to again and again. Here are some ways to cultivate it in daily life:

1. *Recognizing attachment.* Begin by noticing the moments when you think, "I can only be happy if . . ." Pretend this thought is advice from a friend, and decide for yourself if you want to follow it.

2. *Mindful breathing.* When you feel yourself clinging to a specific outcome, pause and take a deep breath. With each exhale, release a little of your attachment to control.

3. *Experiencing a moment without thought.* Find a quiet space and sit with your breath. See if you can experience reality as it is, without any mental story overlaid on top of it.

4. *Practicing gratitude.* Shift your attention from what is missing to what is already here. The present moment holds countless conditions for happiness, if we are willing to see them.

5. *Embracing change.* Remind yourself that everything in life is impermanent. Rather than resisting this truth, practice welcoming it.

THE JOY OF REALITY AS IT IS

The joy of letting go is the joy of freedom. When we release our attachment to how we think things should be, we discover that happiness was never something to be attained—it was always here, waiting to be noticed. Letting go allows us to experience life as it is, full of richness and beauty. It teaches us that reality is not an obstacle to happiness; it is the very source of it.

20

PUPPY MEDITATION
STRENGTHENING

Compassion is one of the most transformative and healing energies that exists. Growing our compassion allows us to respond to suffering with care, kindness, and connection. One of the simplest and most natural ways to tap into compassion is by directing it toward a being that easily elicits feelings of care—such as a puppy or a baby.

A puppy is a perfect example for this practice because most of us instinctively feel kindness and warmth toward small, vulnerable creatures. Their playful innocence, trust, and eagerness for love make it easy for us to send them feelings of care and well-being. However, it is important to remember that this practice can work with any recipient—a loved one, a friend, a pet, or even an image from nature. The key is choosing someone or something that makes it easy to access and nurture the compassionate energy within us.

This practice allows us to strengthen the energy of compassion within ourselves by sending compassion to someone or something that we can't help but love. In choosing the object for your practice, look for an image that brings up feelings that are *strong, positive,* and *uncomplicated*. For example, if you have a lot of love for your mother, but also many other complex feelings, it might be better to choose a puppy.

PRACTICING PUPPY MEDITATION

1. Find a Comfortable Space

Begin by sitting in a comfortable position. Close your eyes, take a deep breath, and allow your body to relax. Let your awareness settle into the present moment.

2. Choose Your Object

Explore different people, animals, and other images until you find one that works for you. For example, you might imagine a small, happy puppy sitting in front of you. See its soft fur, bright eyes, and wagging tail. Picture the way it looks at you with trust and love, simply wanting to be safe, happy, and cared for. Notice how the sensations arise in your body as you focus on this gentle creature. Again, experiment with different images until you find one that is powerful and easy.

3. Generating Compassionate Feelings

As you picture the puppy (or other being), allow the sensations of warmth and kindness to grow within you. Let those sensations be as strong as they want to be. You can try silently repeating phrases such as:

○ "May you be happy."

○ "May you be safe."

○ "May you be loved."

○ "May you be free from suffering."

Feel free to change those phrases or drop them if they don't feel helpful.

Now experiment with imagining a warm, golden light of compassion radiating from your heart, surrounding the puppy (or other being) with love and safety. Feel the connection between your loving-awareness and their openness to receiving it.

4. Expanding the Circle of Compassion

Once you have cultivated a strong feeling of compassion for the puppy (or other being), you can begin expanding this feeling. Picture other puppies, other animals, or people you love. See them basking in the warmth of compassion.

5. Sending Compassion to Yourself

Once you've been practicing puppy meditation for a little while, your body will be filled with oxytocin and other care-related hormones. In that state, you might find it easier to send compassion to yourself. Try this: As you breathe in, imagine receiving the same warmth and kindness that you sent to the puppy. Repeat similar phrases:

○ "May we both be happy."

○ "May we both be safe."

○ "May we both be loved."

Recognize that just as the puppy is deserving of love and care, so are you. Allow yourself to rest in this awareness.

WHY THIS PRACTICE MATTERS

Puppy meditation is a great example of a wholesome pleasure, which is something that feels good in the moment and contributes toward long-term well-being. In Buddhist psychology, our emotions and thoughts are like seeds in the garden of our minds. The more we practice sending compassion, the more we water its seed and the stronger this quality becomes in our daily lives.

When we train in compassion, we also create new neural pathways in the brain that make kindness and patience more natural. We become less reactive and more grounded in warmth and connection. Over time, this practice not only benefits those we send compassion to but also transforms our own inner world, reducing stress and increasing our capacity for love.

BRINGING PUPPY MEDITATION INTO DAILY LIFE

Compassion isn't limited to formal meditation. You can practice puppy meditation throughout your day:

- *Seeing a pet or an animal.* When you see a dog on a walk, silently wish for its happiness and safety.

O *Encountering people.* Whether friends or strangers, take a brief moment to send them silent well-wishes.

O *When feeling stressed.* If you are overwhelmed, pause and recall the warm, effortless compassion you felt for the puppy. Direct it toward yourself in that moment.

21

SUFFERING IN YOUR BODY
ACCEPTANCE

We're learning to see our emotions as seeds in the garden of our minds. Our seed of suffering is like a crying child, in need of our love and attention. If we don't realize that our seed of suffering is present—if we can't hear it crying—we can't care for it appropriately.

The seed of suffering, once activated, doesn't only influence our thoughts. It also manifests as sensations in the body. While it can be really challenging to notice our thoughts without being carried away by them, it's much more possible to track the sensations in our bodies.

When we experience suffering, we can notice it as physical tension, agitation, or heaviness. If the sensations are mild, we recognize that our seed of suffering is present in a small form. If the sensations are overwhelming, we realize that the seed has sprouted powerfully.

Bringing awareness to these sensations is the first step in transforming suffering. Instead of being carried away by distressing thoughts or emotional reactivity, we gently bring our attention back to the body and notice what is happening without judgment.

MINDFULNESS OF SUFFERING

Mindfulness of suffering begins with paying close attention to the sensations in your body throughout the day. This includes both formal meditation periods as well as moments of reflection as you move through daily life. The body holds suffering in ways we often don't recognize: tension in the shoulders, heaviness in the chest, tightness in the jaw, a sense of shakiness in the stomach. These physical signals reveal when our seed of suffering has been activated.

COMPASSION FOR THE BODY'S SUFFERING

Once we recognize the presence of suffering in our body, we practice meeting it with compassion. Instead of resisting the discomfort or wishing it away, we acknowledge its presence with kindness. The tension, the heaviness, the agitation—these are energies in need of love.

One simple practice is to pause and say to yourself, "I am here for you." Imagine sending warmth and care to the places of suffering in your body, as if you were comforting a dear friend. If it helps, place a gentle hand over the area where you feel distress and allow the warmth of your own touch to provide comfort.

WORKING WITH INTENSITY: THE 3-TO-7 RULE

When bringing mindfulness to suffering, it is helpful to gauge its intensity. On a scale of 0 to 10, where 0 is no suffering and 10 is the worst you've ever felt, aim to keep your distress within the 3-to-7 range. If the suffering is mild, you can observe it with ease. If it rises beyond a 7, it may become too overwhelming to meet with loving-awareness. In such cases, it is okay to step back, focus on the breath, and find a grounding practice before returning to the sensations in the body.

This approach allows us to gradually build our capacity to hold suffering without becoming overwhelmed. Over time, our ability to remain present with discomfort increases, and our reactions become less intense.

A PRACTICE FOR HOLDING SUFFERING IN THE BODY

Try this practice when you notice any distress in your body:

1. *Pause and breathe.* Stop what you are doing and take a deep, slow breath.

2. *Scan your body.* Gently bring your attention to any sensations of tension, tightness, or discomfort.

3. *Acknowledge with kindness.* Instead of pushing the sensations away, softly say, "I see you. I am here for you."

4. *Send compassion.* Imagine sending warmth and care to the part of your body that holds suffering. If helpful, place a hand over the area as a gesture of support.

5. *Allow and observe.* Let the sensations be present without needing to change them. Notice how they shift over time.

HEALING THROUGH AWARENESS

By regularly practicing mindfulness of suffering in the body, we strengthen our capacity for inner peace. We learn that suffering is not something to be feared or avoided but something that can be held with love. As we develop this ability, the seed of suffering loses its power, and the seed of loving-awareness grows stronger in its place. In this way, we create the conditions for deep healing, allowing us to move through life with greater ease and compassion.

TRANSFORMATION
AT THE BASE
TRANSFORMING

In the garden of our minds, every possible mental state exists in the form of seeds—a seed of suffering, a seed of joy, and others seeds of deep insight and peace. When we bring mindfulness and loving-awareness into our practice, we engage in an ancient process of transformation, one that Buddhist teachers have described for over 2,000 years.

One of the earliest metaphors for this process comes from ancient India, where fragrant flowers like jasmine were placed in a box with sesame seeds. Over time, the fragrance infused into the seeds, changing their flavor. This is how loving-awareness works—it doesn't erase a painful experience from the past but infuses it with warmth and healing.

BALANCING TWO SEEDS

Sometimes the seed of suffering will manifest in our mind, often in the form of fear, anger, or sadness. When that happens, it's possible to invite the seed of loving-awareness to manifest alongside it. Those two energies don't cancel each other out—they interact. When suffering meets love, it begins to change.

The practice here is to invite suffering to manifest—but only as much as we can hold with care. If it becomes overwhelming, we step back and focus on strengthening positive seeds before returning. Healing is not about force; it's about balance.

THE PRACTICE OF INVITING TWO SEEDS

To begin, settle into a quiet place where you feel safe and supported. Take a few deep breaths, feeling the ground beneath you. Before we engage with our suffering, we must also invite the presence of our own strength and love.

1. *Choose your level of intensity.* Only invite the level of suffering that you can hold with kindness. If the intensity of suffering rises beyond a 7 on a scale of 1–10, shift your focus to cultivating positive seeds first. Be careful not to overwhelm yourself; healing happens in waves, not in floods.

2. *Call forth the seed of suffering.* Close your eyes and bring to mind an experience of fear, anger, sorrow, or anxiety— something that feels alive but not overwhelming. Notice its presence in your body. Does it bring images, words, or colors alongside the bodily sensations? It's

okay to notice everything that arises, but be careful not to lose touch with your body.

3. *Now invite loving-awareness.* Just as gently as you invited suffering, now call forth the seed of loving-awareness. Imagine it as a fragrant flower blooming in your heart, filling your body with warmth, compassion, and deep care. Let it expand around the suffering, not to suppress it but to meet it with tenderness.

4. *Observe the infusion process.* Picture the suffering and loving-awareness sitting together, just as the sesame seed and the jasmine flower rest in the same box. What happens when love meets fear? When compassion meets sorrow? Pay special attention to the sensations in your body.

5. *Stay with the process.* Allow yourself to be with this alchemical process as long as it feels nourishing. If suffering feels too intense, gently return to the fragrance of loving-awareness alone. You can flip to another section of this book that focuses on cultivating positive seeds.

HOLDING BOTH WITHOUT
BEING OVERWHELMED

One of the greatest skills we can develop is the ability to hold suffering without being carried away by it. In Buddhist psychology, this is known as mindfulness of suffering. Just as a gardener knows how much water and sunlight each plant needs, we must learn how much suffering we can hold without being overwhelmed.

If at any moment suffering feels too strong, turn your attention to something soothing—perhaps recalling a moment of kindness, gratitude, or joy. Let the fragrance of loving-awareness fill more space before returning to the seed of suffering. Healing is a process of rhythm, of knowing when to sit with suffering and when to step back and cultivate joy.

LONG-TERM CHANGE

With time, this practice changes the way suffering lives inside of us. A pain that once felt sharp and isolating becomes something we can hold with grace. Fear that once contracted the body begins to loosen its grip. The nervous system learns that it is safe to experience pain without being consumed by it.

This is the power of transformation at the base. We do not need to remove suffering to be free—rather, we allow loving-awareness to infuse it with new meaning. Just as the fragrance of jasmine transforms the sesame seed, love transforms fear, presence transforms pain, and compassion transforms even the heaviest burdens into something we can carry with wisdom and care.

Through this practice, we learn that our suffering is not a sign of failure, nor is it something we must escape. It is an invitation—a doorway to healing—waiting for us to meet it with love.

23

THE PEOPLE
WHO'VE TREATED
YOU BADLY
TRANSFORMING

We don't just carry memories of specific experiences—we also carry the people who have impacted us. The voices of our parents, teachers, friends, and everyone who has helped us or hurt us don't just fade into the past. They live within us as networks of neurons, shaping our thoughts, feelings, and sense of self. When these relationships remain unresolved their weight burdens us in the present. But we have the power to change how they live inside us.

Whenever someone treats us badly, it affects us in two ways. First, there is the direct pain of feeling unloved, disrespected, or misunderstood. The hurt, disappointment, and anger leave an imprint. And there's a second layer—a story we tell ourselves about why the other person acted that way. We're rarely aware of the stories we create, but they are easily found if we scratch just below the surface.

If we were young and the person was important, like a parent or caregiver, we may have blamed ourselves. One child might assume *If they are treating me this way, it must be how I deserve to be treated.* For another child it can be *The only way to keep our connection is to believe you're right to treat me like this.* And for another child it's *If this is my fault, then I could make it stop by becoming better.* Whatever story goes along with the experience, over time it takes root, shaping our self-worth and the way we relate to others.

PRACTICING WITH UNRESOLVED PAIN

Healing doesn't require that we confront or change the other person. It comes from transforming how their presence lives within us. The core practice is to bring awareness to the suffering, allow it to be there, and hold it with love and compassion.

Step 1: Inviting the Memory to Arise

Find a quiet place where you feel safe. Close your eyes and take a few breaths, allowing your body to settle. Bring to mind someone who has treated you badly. It could be a parent, a teacher, a peer—anyone whose words or actions left a lasting imprint.

Picture them in your mind. You are not engaging with them or trying to change them. You are simply allowing their presence to arise. As you hold their image, notice what happens in your body. Where do you feel the impact of this relationship? Maybe there is tightness in your chest, heaviness in your stomach, or tension in your jaw. Whatever arises, let it be there.

Step 2: Feeling the Suffering

For a few breaths, stay with the physical sensations. You are not analyzing or justifying—just feeling. Acknowledge the hurt, the injustice, the longing for things to have been different. If self-blame arises, recognize it as part of the old conditioning. You were never responsible for another person's unkindness. As much as you can, stay focused on the suffering as sensation in the body. This will help you avoid being carried away by stories.

Step 3: Bringing in Compassion

Now, direct the energy of warmth and care toward your suffering. There are different ways to do this:

○ *Send love to yourself.* Imagine wrapping your younger self in warmth and kindness. You might silently say, "You deserved love. You deserved kindness. You are good and whole just as you are."

○ *Invite a compassionate presence.* If it feels difficult to generate warmth for yourself, picture someone else who embodies love and wisdom: a spiritual figure, a kind friend, a beloved pet. Let them sit beside you, radiating acceptance and comfort.

○ *Let the suffering be held.* See what happens if you visualize love pervading everywhere in the world, and always ready to hold your suffering. Imagine that love and warmth gently infusing the tightness in your body, softening the pain at its own pace.

○ *Changing the story.* Speak to your younger self and help them understand why this *actually* happened. It might be that the other person was in a lot of pain or didn't understand how to be kinder. Explain to your younger self that you always deserved love, even when other people were hurtful.

Step 4: Letting Go of the Other Person

You are not here to forgive, explain, or change the other person. They are simply there, in your awareness, without needing anything from you. If the impulse to forgive arises naturally, let it happen. But do not force it. Forgiveness is admirable, but it's not the goal of this particular practice—healing is. Keep focusing on the suffering in your body until it feels lighter, more open, and a sense of sweetness begins to emerge.

HOW THIS PRACTICE CHANGES YOU

Each time you do this, you reshape how these unresolved relationships live inside you. The weight they carried begins to soften. Instead of being a raw wound, the memory becomes something you can hold with kindness. The people who have treated you badly lose their grip on your present self.

You are not erasing the past, nor are you pretending that harm didn't happen. You are changing how it affects you now. The more you practice, the more space you create for peace, resilience, and genuine freedom.

24

FULL AWARENESS
OF BREATHING: PART I
SUTRA STUDY

The first part of the *Sutra on the Full Awareness of Breathing* focuses on the body. These initial four exercises are designed to develop mindfulness of breath, expand awareness to the entire body, and cultivate a sense of calm. Together, they serve as a foundation for developing deep presence and for healing trauma.

EXERCISES 1–4

1 and 2. Knowing a Long or Short Breath

> "Breathing in a long breath, I know I am breathing
> in a long breath. Breathing out a long breath,
> I know I am breathing out a long breath."

"Breathing in a short breath, I know I am breathing in a short breath. Breathing out a short breath, I know I am breathing out a short breath."

Although these are taught as Exercises 1 and 2, they really

go together. In this sutra, we begin with a narrow focus: simply observing the breath as it is. Whether the breath is long or short, we don't try to change it. Instead, we witness the natural rhythm of the body's breathing. This is an essential first step in healing because it allows us to cultivate nonjudgmental, open awareness. Trauma often leaves us disconnected from our own bodily sensations, either avoiding them or trying to control them. Here, we practice simply allowing the breath to happen, as it is, without resistance. We're building a sense of trust in our body's natural processes.

You might focus your awareness on your chest, on your nose, or both. The important part is the sense of trust that you build through the practice of letting your body breathe without trying to control anything.

3. Awareness of the Whole Body

> "Breathing in, I am aware of my whole body.
> Breathing out, I am aware of my whole body."

After grounding our awareness in the breath, we expand it to encompass the entire body. There are more sensations happening in your body at each moment than you could ever count. As you try to become consciously aware of them, they will completely fill your field of awareness. From this state, it's impossible to be lost in thought because there isn't any more room.

We practice witnessing our body as a whole, which includes all pleasant, unpleasant, and neutral sensations.

For those healing from trauma, this is another vital practice. The process of feeling sensations in the body without attempting to control them builds an even deeper sense of faith in ourselves.

The body also holds unprocessed experiences, and bringing gentle awareness to it allows us to begin reintegrating those experiences safely. Many of us have learned to tune out physical sensations, but here we create space to reconnect without judgment or control.

You can stay with this practice as long as you'd like. Sometimes it can be helpful to practice like this for weeks at a time before moving to the next exercise.

4. Calming the Whole Body

> "Breathing in, I calm my whole body.
> Breathing out, I calm my whole body."

Once we have learned to observe the body passively, we take the next step: actively cultivating calm. While the first three exercises teach us to witness, this step teaches us how to influence our internal state with kindness. Healing trauma involves learning both passive observation and active cultivation. By gently calming the body, we tell our nervous system that it is safe to relax.

This is not forced relaxation but a natural unfolding, and it absolutely must come *after* the first three. As we bring awareness to the breath and body, a sense of ease arises on its own. When we soften the tension we find, we develop trust in our ability to regulate ourselves. Over time, this leads to greater resilience, allowing us to respond to challenges with more steadiness and ease.

THE BALANCE OF PASSIVE
AND ACTIVE PRACTICE

These four practices form a progression, moving from simple awareness of breath to a broader awareness of the body, and finally to intentional calming. Healing requires both acceptance and transformation. We begin by simply seeing what is present inside of ourselves, and creating space for all the sensations we find. Only once we have cultivated that space do we gently intervene, guiding the body toward calmness.

Through this process, we develop a vital skill: the ability to stay present with ourselves. Whether we are experiencing discomfort, fear, or ease, we learn to meet it all with mindfulness.

25

FULL AWARENESS OF
BREATHING: PART II
SUTRA STUDY

The next four exercises of the *Sutra on the Full Awareness of Breathing* guide us in working with our emotions. Building on the foundation of breath and body awareness, we now cultivate positive emotional states, observe difficult emotions as they arise, and learn to calm them. These practices help us deepen our emotional intelligence and resilience.

EXERCISES 5–8

5. Cultivating Joy

"Breathing in, I feel joyful. Breathing out, I feel joyful."

Joy in Buddhist practice is an active state of upliftment, carrying an element of lightness and enthusiasm. This practice is an opportunity to connect with what brings us joy and to strengthen those positive seeds. Instead of waiting for joy to arise spontaneously, we actively cultivate it.

To practice this, you can recall a time when you felt deeply joyful—perhaps in nature, with a loved one, or engaged in an activity you love. Let that memory nourish you as you breathe in and out. The more we practice returning to joy, the more accessible it becomes, even in difficult moments. For trauma healing, this practice strengthens the capacity to hold positivity alongside suffering, preventing us from becoming stuck in pain.

6. Cultivating Happiness

"Breathing in, I feel happy. Breathing out, I feel happy."

Happiness is distinct from joy in Buddhist philosophy. Where joy has an energetic, excited quality, happiness is a deeper state of contentment and peace. This practice allows us to cultivate a sense of ease and fulfillment.

As you breathe, bring to mind something that creates a feeling of deep happiness—perhaps a sense of belonging, gratitude, or simply being alive in this moment. This practice teaches us that happiness is not dependent on external circumstances; it can be cultivated internally. As we heal from trauma, this can be a profound shift: learning that well-being is possible in this moment.

7. Becoming Aware of Emotions

"Breathing in, I am aware of my emotions.
Breathing out, I am aware of my emotions."

This practice moves from cultivating positive emotions to observing all emotions, without trying to change them. The experience of bathing in joy and happiness has prepared us for whatever other emotions might want to arise, including painful ones. Instead of suppressing or controlling what arises, we allow whatever emotions that want to come up to fully surface. This creates what can be called *psychological circulation*: allowing emotions to move freely rather than become stagnant or repressed.

For those carrying trauma, emotions may feel overwhelming or difficult to approach. This practice strengthens our ability to sit with them without fear. Simply observe: What is present? Sadness? Fear? Anger? Peace? Let any emotion arise and pass like clouds in the sky, knowing that none of them define you. This step is crucial because it builds trust in ourselves—showing us that we can feel our emotions deeply and still remain grounded.

8. Calming Emotions

> "Breathing in, I calm my emotions.
> Breathing out, I calm my emotions."

Having observed emotions without resistance, we now move toward soothing them. Exercises 7 and 8 mirror the progression of Exercises 3 and 4: first passive observation, then active cultivation.

Imagine your emotions as waves on the ocean. Some may be turbulent, others gentle, but all can be softened by the energy of love. As you breathe in, acknowledge whatever emotion is present. As you breathe out, send a sense of calm and reassurance to yourself. You might use a phrase like "It's okay. I am here for you."

For trauma healing, this step is vital. It shows us that it is possible to respond skillfully to any emotion that might arise. We don't need to be afraid that painful feelings might bubble to the surface, because we've learned how to care for them. Over time, this practice rewires our relationship to emotions, allowing us to meet them with kindness instead of fear.

BALANCING JOY, AWARENESS, AND SOOTHING

Together, these four exercises create a balanced approach to working with emotions. First, we strengthen positive emotions (joy and happiness), which builds our internal resources. Then, we allow any emotions to surface without resistance, increasing self-trust. Finally, we learn how to calm and regulate emotions, giving us a sense of agency over our inner world.

Through these practices, we come to understand that emotions are not problems to fix but energies to hold with mindfulness. We do not need to fear them or suppress them. Instead, we meet them with curiosity, kindness, and skillful care, transforming the way we experience both joy and suffering in our lives.

26

FULL AWARENESS
OF BREATHING: PART III
SUTRA STUDY

The next section of the *Sutra on the Full Awareness of Breathing* shifts focus from the body and emotions to the mind itself. These four exercises guide us through mental awareness, cultivating happiness, deep concentration, and ultimately, liberation. By working skillfully with our thoughts, we strengthen our capacity for healing, insight, and freedom.

EXERCISES 9–12

9. Becoming Aware of the Mind

> "Breathing in, I am aware of my mind.
> Breathing out, I am aware of my mind."

This practice begins with simple observation. Just as we previously observed the breath, body, and emotions, we now turn our attention to the mind. Thoughts, perceptions, and mental states arise and pass, like clouds moving through the sky. Instead of being carried away or trying to control them, we allow them to come and go freely.

This is a practice of *mental circulation*: giving space to all thoughts rather than suppressing some while clinging to others. Just as emotions need to flow in order to be fully processed, thoughts need movement to avoid becoming stuck in rigid patterns. By developing awareness of the mind, we learn that we are not our thoughts. Instead, we are the observer, capable of witnessing them with clarity and ease.

10. Cultivating a Happy Mind

"Breathing in, I make my mind happy.
Breathing out, I make my mind happy."

Once we have allowed thoughts to circulate freely, we intentionally shift our thinking toward happiness. This is not about denial or forced positivity—it is about realizing that we have the power to shape our perspective. Just as a garden holds many different seeds, our mind holds many different ways of seeing.

We ask ourselves: "What ways of thinking bring happiness?" and "What perspectives create lightness and ease?" Instead of being trapped by negative or habitual thinking, we actively cultivate optimism. This doesn't mean ignoring our pain but rather recognizing that even within suffering, there are seeds of happiness waiting to be watered. This practice strengthens resilience, allowing us to meet difficulties with greater steadiness.

11. Concentrating the Mind

"Breathing in, I concentrate my mind.
Breathing out, I concentrate my mind."

A concentrated mind is a powerful mind. This practice builds on the previous exercises by training us to stay present without distraction. We direct our awareness fully to the present moment, observing what is here without being pulled into mental stories or wandering thoughts.

Concentration gives us stability. When the mind is scattered, we feel weak and ungrounded. But when the mind is focused, there is a deep sense of strength and clarity. This is the foundation for insight and transformation—when we can fully hold our attention in the present, we see things as they truly are.

12. Liberating the Mind

"Breathing in, I liberate my mind.
Breathing out, I liberate my mind."

Liberation comes when we let go of mental attachments: stories, beliefs, and perceptions that keep us stuck. This does not mean rejecting our experiences but freeing ourselves from being controlled by them. Many of our thoughts are rooted in misunderstandings or outdated narratives about who we are and what is possible.

To liberate the mind is to see clearly. We let go of what no longer serves us and step fully into reality as it is. We are not bound by the past nor anxious about the future. We are here, awake, and free.

STRENGTHENING THE MIND FOR HEALING

Together, these four exercises form a powerful process. We begin with awareness, learning to observe the mind without grasping or avoiding. Then we cultivate happiness, choosing perspectives that nourish us. We build focus, concentrating our energy and attention. Finally, we free ourselves from limiting thoughts and perceptions, stepping into a more expansive way of being.

Trauma often leaves us stuck in cycles of thought that reinforce fear, self-doubt, or despair. By training the mind through these exercises, we learn to loosen those patterns. We develop the ability to hold both suffering and joy, to focus deeply, and ultimately to let go of what no longer supports our well-being.

These practices remind us that true freedom is not just about external circumstances—it is about how we relate to our own mind. When we learn to observe, cultivate, concentrate, and liberate, we move forward in life not just as survivors but as free people, fully present and empowered in our own experience.

27

FULL AWARENESS
OF BREATHING: PART IV
SUTRA STUDY

The last four exercises of the *Sutra on the Full Awareness of Breathing* guide us into the deepest dimensions of practice. Having cultivated awareness of the body, emotions, and mind, we now turn to the nature of reality itself. These final practices invite us to directly experience impermanence, the fading of desire, the insight of no birth and no death, and the ultimate freedom of letting go.

EXERCISES 13–16

13. Observing Impermanence

"Breathing in, I observe the impermanent nature of all phenomena. Breathing out, I observe the impermanent nature of all phenomena."

In this practice, we turn our awareness to the truth that all things— our thoughts, emotions, bodies, and even the universe itself—are in a constant state of transformation. There is nothing we experience that remains the same from one moment to the next.

We can observe this directly, as we take a breath in. An oxygen molecule that you inhale was floating through the atmosphere. Prior to that, it was part of a leaf, and long ago, it was part of another person's body. Now it's part of yours. The water in your body was once rain, then a river, then a cup of tea. That water and oxygen has been water and oxygen since the earth was formed, and will be for millions of years into the future. Even your thoughts are made out of language that has been evolving as long as people have been speaking. This deep understanding of impermanence helps loosen our grasp on things we mistakenly believe to be fixed, whether it's our pain, our identity, or our attachments.

14. Observing the Disappearance of Desire

"Breathing in, I observe the disappearance of desire.
Breathing out, I observe the disappearance of desire."

As we recognize impermanence, our craving and aversion begin to lose their hold. We chase after things—relationships, achievements, possessions—because we believe they will complete us. But when we see deeply into impermanence, we realize there is nothing to cling to, because everything is already changing.

Desire fades naturally when we stop feeding it. Instead of seeking happiness in something external, we find that peace is already available when we stop grasping. In this practice, we observe how desires arise and dissolve on their own. As we breathe, we witness them appearing and vanishing, like ripples in a pond.

15. Observing No Birth, No Death

> "Breathing in, I observe the no-birth, no-death
> nature of all phenomena. Breathing out, I observe
> the no-birth, no-death nature of all phenomena."

This practice leads us beyond ordinary concepts of existence. In Buddhism, birth and death are just convenient designations. If everything is in a state of transformation, nothing ever truly begins or ends. What we call "birth" is simply the continuation of conditions that came before, and what we call "death" is just another transformation.

A cloud does not die when it becomes rain; it transforms. While you might be able to say that a specific wave on the ocean has a moment it began and a moment it crashed on the shore, it has always been made of water, which has always been moving and changing.

In the same way, when we look deeply at ourselves, we see that we are not bound by birth or death. The body changes, the mind changes, but nothing is ever truly lost. If we can see this deeply, we no longer fear death—because we understand that there is no real ending, only continuation. This insight can bring immense freedom and peace.

16. Observing Letting Go

> "Breathing in, I observe letting go.
> Breathing out, I observe letting go."

With insight into impermanence and no birth, no death, we come to the final practice: complete letting go. Letting go does not mean rejecting life or becoming indifferent. It means fully trusting the natural flow of existence, no longer trying to control or hold on to anything.

We let go of our expectations. We let go of our grasping. We let go of the need to make things different than they are. In doing so, we open ourselves completely to the beauty of the present moment.

This is the ultimate freedom—not being bound by fear, not being caught in craving, not clinging to identity or the past. It is a return to reality exactly as it is, with nothing added, nothing taken away. This is true peace.

THE PATH OF DEEP LIBERATION

These final four exercises bring the *Sutra on the Full Awareness of Breathing* to its highest point. First, we witness the reality of impermanence. Then, we see how this truth dissolves our attachments and desires. With deeper insight, we recognize that birth and death are illusions, and finally, we let go completely, stepping into boundless freedom.

This is not just philosophy—it is something we can experience directly. By practicing awareness in this way, we reshape our perception of life itself. We release suffering at its root, not by running from it, but by seeing deeply into its nature.

Through these exercises, we train ourselves to walk through the world with lightness, free from the weight of illusions, embracing life as a continuous, flowing miracle.

28

THE SUFFERING
OF MY FAMILY
AND FRIENDS
COMPASSIONATE ACTION

As we deepen our practice of responding to our own suffering with compassion and acceptance, we naturally begin to extend that same understanding to others. We recognize that when people act out in anger, fear, or unkindness, they are not simply choosing to be difficult—they are suffering. Instead of reacting with frustration or resentment, we begin to see their pain.

Think about a time in the recent past when you were upset with someone in your life. Maybe they spoke to you harshly, ignored you, or acted selfishly. Now, instead of focusing on how they hurt you, ask: "Can I see the suffering that was present in them?" and "What pain might they have been carrying?" When we look deeply, we see that suffering is always the absence of love and understanding. As we cultivate the ability to meet our own pain with kindness, it starts to feel natural to do the same for others.

WELCOMING THE SUFFERING OF OTHERS

This does not mean we passively accept harmful behavior. But it does mean we are no longer afraid of emotions like anger, grief, or frustration—whether in ourselves or in others. We have learned to sit with these feelings in our own practice, to breathe with them, to welcome them instead of resisting them. And so, when we see them arise in another person, we don't need to react with defensiveness or withdrawal. Instead, we can acknowledge: *This person is suffering*.

This shift in perception changes everything. Instead of taking things personally, we become curious. Instead of judgment, we feel compassion. Our relationships begin to soften, and we find that even small acts of patience and understanding can bring relief to those around us.

LOVING WITH BOUNDARIES

Recognizing that someone is suffering doesn't mean we must accept harmful behavior. My first meditation teacher, Joanne Friday, once told me: "It is your practice to love everyone, but you don't need to take them home with you." Love doesn't mean sacrificing our well-being. Some people's suffering is expressed in ways that are destructive, manipulative, or unkind. In these cases, we can hold compassion for them, but we can also set boundaries.

We can love someone from afar. We can wish them peace without inviting them into our inner circle. We can say *no* with kindness, knowing that taking care of ourselves is also a way of taking care of the world. Sometimes, the most loving thing we can do is to protect our own peace.

SENDING LOVE TO THE COLLECTIVE SUFFERING OF THE WORLD

Beyond the suffering of individuals, we can recognize the immense suffering that exists in the world. The weight of war, injustice, illness, and loss can feel overwhelming, but we do not have to carry it alone. Instead, we can send love and acceptance into the collective suffering of the world.

Take a moment now. Close your eyes, breathe deeply, and silently offer this wish:

May all beings who are suffering find relief.

May those consumed by anger find peace.

May those lost in fear find safety.

May those overwhelmed by grief find comfort.

This practice reminds us that we are never separate from the suffering of others, nor from the love that has the power to heal it. Through awareness, compassion, and the wisdom to set boundaries when needed, we can walk the path of understanding—not just for ourselves but for the world around us.

FOURTH CYCLE

29

GETTING TO KNOW
YOUR THOUGHTS
STRENGTHENING

The human mind is an incredible gift. It is constantly working—generating thoughts, interpreting the world, and trying to guide us toward safety and happiness. In Buddhism, we say that the mind is made of Buddha nature, which means its deepest intention is compassionate. However, we also say that the mind is conditioned by ignorance. This means that the mind's motivation might be to avoid harm and seek well-being, but that much of the time, it doesn't know how to do that effectively.

Understanding our thoughts is an essential part of our journey toward greater clarity and healing. If we can observe our minds with curiosity rather than judgment, we begin to see how our thoughts are shaped by both compassion and misunderstanding. As we get to know our thoughts, we cultivate a healthier relationship with them—one that allows us to listen with kindness, discern their value, and choose which ones to follow.

BUDDHA NATURE: THE DEEPEST
MOTIVATION OF THE MIND

One of the easiest ways to recognize Buddha nature is to observe the simplest forms of life. Consider a single-celled organism. It moves toward food and away from toxins. Every living being, from an amoeba to a human, is trying to meet its needs and avoid harm. This motivation is not something we consciously create; it is inherent to being alive.

It's possible to see this deep motivation in our minds. We instinctively seek happiness, security, and well-being. We want to feel loved, respected, and safe. We want to avoid pain, fear, and suffering. This is the essence of Buddha nature—the fundamental desire for wholeness and peace. No matter how confused or reactive we may become, at the root of every thought and action is the basic drive to protect ourselves and seek happiness.

IGNORANCE: WHEN WE DON'T KNOW
HOW TO HELP OURSELVES

While our Buddha nature seeks well-being, ignorance often distorts our ability to reach it. Ignorance (*avidya*), in the Buddhist sense, doesn't mean stupidity. It simply means not knowing, or more literally, not seeing. Life seeks flourishing, but we just don't know how to accomplish it.

For example, imagine you're driving in traffic and another driver cuts you off. Your immediate reaction might be anger. You might even roll down your window and scream at them. Take a moment and imagine doing something like that. What would be motivating you? Maybe their actions felt unsafe and disrespectful. Upon reflection, you might see that your deep motivation was your need to feel safe and respected. However, it's obvious that throwing a temper tantrum on the highway doesn't make you any safer or make anyone more likely to respect you. This is an example of our Buddha nature being conditioned by ignorance—our intention is to meet our needs, but we lack the insight to act in a way that actually benefits us.

Every living thing shares in this predicament. We all want to be free from suffering, but we often don't know how. Instead, we react, driven by habitual patterns that don't serve us. Recognizing this universal struggle can lead us to a greater sense of compassion— not just for ourselves but for everyone around us.

THE PURPOSE OF THINKING

One of the primary functions of the mind is to look at the present moment and imagine how things could be better or safer. For example, when your stomach feels the sensation of hunger, your mind immediately starts generating images of what kind of food you might want to eat. If you feel lonely, your mind may begin planning how to reach out to a friend. This is the mind's attempt to be helpful.

As mentioned earlier, it can be useful to think of the mind like a well-meaning but sometimes misguided friend. Imagine sitting across from a friend who always offers advice, whether you want it or not. Sometimes the advice is helpful and insightful. Sometimes your friend misunderstands your situation entirely. And sometimes, you simply don't need any advice at all.

This is how our thoughts function. They arise spontaneously, offering suggestions, predictions, and interpretations. Some thoughts are useful, others are misleading, and many are simply habitual patterns. Learning to observe these thoughts rather than immediately believing or acting on them is a powerful step toward wisdom.

DIFFERENTIATING BETWEEN SENSATIONS AND THOUGHTS

One of the most important skills in working with the mind is learning to differentiate between the *sensations in the body* and the *thoughts that arise along with them*.

Sensations are direct physical experiences: tightness in the chest, warmth in the belly, tension in the shoulders. Thoughts, on the other hand, can be seen as the advice our mind is offering us, or stories we're creating about what's happening. For example, a feeling of tightness in the chest might be accompanied by the thought "I'm not good enough" or "Something terrible is going to happen."

By learning to separate sensation from thought, we can observe our emotions without getting caught in a cycle of distress. The next time you experience a strong emotion, try this:

○ Pause and take a breath.

○ Notice what is happening in your body. Where do you feel the emotion?

○ Label the sensation without attaching meaning. For

example: *There is tightness in my chest* rather than *I'm so anxious.*

○ Recognize any accompanying thoughts. Are they helpful? Are they true?

This practice helps us become more aware of how the mind reacts to bodily sensations, allowing us to respond with greater clarity rather than being pulled into emotional reactivity.

PRACTICING THOUGHT AWARENESS

One of the simplest and most profound practices in Buddhism is learning to observe your thoughts. Instead of identifying with your thoughts or feeling compelled to act on them, you can learn to see them for what they are.

Try this practice:

○ Find a quiet place to sit comfortably.

○ Close your eyes and take a few deep breaths.

○ Notice the thoughts that arise in your mind.

○ Rather than following each thought, imagine that you are simply listening.

○ If a thought suggests action, recognize that it's just a thought—not an order.

○ If a thought is judging or narrating something in your life, recognize that it's just a thought—not ultimate reality.

○ Ask yourself: "Is this thought helpful? Is it wise? Do I need to act on it right now?"

The goal is not to suppress or stop thoughts. Instead, it is about developing a mindful relationship with them: acknowledging them, understanding them, and deciding whether or not to engage with them.

Getting to know your thoughts is one of the most powerful ways to cultivate mindfulness and self-awareness. By understanding that your mind's deepest motivation is always to seek well-being, you can relate to your thoughts with greater patience and compassion.

Rather than being caught in cycles of reactivity, you can step back and observe your thoughts like a kind and understanding friend. You can recognize when thoughts are helpful and when they are misleading. And most importantly, you can learn that you are not your thoughts by connecting with the awareness that sees them and the wisdom that chooses how to respond.

With practice, this shift in perspective can transform the way you experience yourself and the world around you.

30

RECEIVING COMPASSION FROM OTHERS
STRENGTHENING

In the traditional Buddhist text, the *Visuddhimagga*, the renowned teacher Buddhaghosa describes how we can develop the quality of compassion in order to heal and liberate ourselves. One of the main principles is that we begin with a practice that's easy for us, and then progress toward more difficult practices.

For some of us, the easiest practice is to receive love and compassion from someone else. If that's true for you, this will be a great way to start. However, many other people find it difficult to receive compassion, and it's much easier to send it to others. This obstacle can stem from past wounds, feelings of unworthiness, or a deep-seated belief that we must bear our struggles alone. However, learning to receive compassion is something we always can work toward, even if it's not easy.

WHY RECEIVING COMPASSION CAN BE DIFFICULT

Many of us have been conditioned to believe that relying on others is a sign of weakness. We might fear being a burden, or we may struggle to trust that others genuinely want to support us. Trauma, in particular, can reinforce these fears, making us hesitant to let down our defenses and accept help. The very experiences that made us long for kindness and connection may have also taught us that such gestures come with conditions or risks.

Yet, compassion is too important to our healing for us to allow that to be the end of the story. In the decades I've spent teaching self-compassion, I've come to believe that everyone can find some way to get in touch with the energy of compassion and direct it toward their suffering. The practice of receiving compassion from someone else might not be the best path for you, but it also might be. Give it a try and see how it feels.

PRACTICES FOR RECEIVING COMPASSION

1. Visualizing Compassion From a Loving Presence

A powerful way to open ourselves to compassion is through visualization. In this practice, we imagine a source of kindness and care directing warmth and love toward us. This presence can take many forms:

○ A close friend or family member

○ A spiritual figure, such as the Buddha, Jesus, or another being who embodies love

○ A beloved pet

○ Even an image from nature, such as the warmth of the sun or a beautiful tree

Try This Practice

1. Close your eyes and take a few deep breaths.

Picture this compassionate presence before you.

Imagine them offering you kind words, a reassuring smile, or some other form of compassion. For example, they might say:

   ○ "May you be loved."
   ○ "May you be safe."
   ○ "May you feel at ease."
   ○ "May you be happy."

2. As you breathe in, allow yourself to receive this love.
   As you breathe out, direct that love to the exact place inside you that needs it most.

This exercise can help grow our capacity to be more receptive to the care that is available to us.

2. Feeling Compassion in the Body

Compassion is not just an idea—it is something we feel in the body. When we allow ourselves to receive kindness, there are physical sensations that accompany the experience: warmth in the chest, relaxation in the shoulders, a deep sense of comfort.

Try This Practice

1. Bring back the image from the last practice.
   Let the image become very clear.

2. Allow that being to send love and care to you.
   See if you can let it in.

3. As you practice, notice how your body responds.
   Do you feel a softening or an opening?

4. Allow yourself to feel this sensation. Recognize that compassion is not something we must grasp for—it is something we can simply allow.

3. Accepting Kindness Without Deflection

Now we're going to practice being more open to receiving compassion in your daily life. So many of us deflect kindness from the people in our lives. We might ignore it because we feel like the kindness doesn't make up for other negative things the person has done. We might not feel like we deserve it, or we might not be paying attention. In this practice, we work on allowing ourselves to be nourished by even small acts of kindness.

To shift this habit:

○ Find a quiet place to sit or lie down.

○ Remember a recent time that someone offered you a compliment or an act of kindness. It can be small or large. It might just be someone treating you with basic human decency. Picture yourself in that scene, and pause right there.

○ Notice the feelings arising in your body, and let yourself feel them. You might notice alarm, warmth, or even both. Allow the feelings to come and go however they want to.

○ Imagine yourself simply saying, "Thank you," if that feels appropriate. Stay with the feelings in your body.

○ Notice how it feels to fully receive what is being offered without minimizing it.

This practice may seem small, but over time it can significantly change how we relate to compassion.

THE HEALING POWER OF RECEIVING COMPASSION

Healing happens when our suffering makes contact with compassion. The practice of receiving compassion can be a helpful way to grow our capacity to get in touch with the energy of compassion. Receiving compassion is an acknowledgment that we, like everyone else, are worthy of kindness. The more we practice receiving, the more we recognize that compassion is not scarce—it is abundant, always available, and waiting for us to accept it.

INTEGRATING THIS PRACTICE INTO DAILY LIFE

○ *Practice receiving small acts of kindness.* Whether it's a smile from a stranger or someone holding the door for you, let these moments in.

○ *Reflect on past moments of compassion.* Spend time remembering times when you have been supported, and recognize that these experiences are real.

○ *Ask for help when needed.* Seeking support is not a weakness but a recognition of our shared humanity.

○ *Surround yourself with compassionate people.* Create relationships that encourage mutual care and kindness.

31

THE FOUR NUTRIMENTS
STRENGTHENING

Just as our physical bodies require nourishment, so too do our emotional and mental states. The Buddha taught that everything we consume—physically, emotionally, and mentally—is a type of nutriment.

The Buddha described four types of *nutriments*, or foods:

○ *Edible food.* The food we eat.

○ *Sensory impressions.* Everything we take into our consciousness through our senses.

○ *Volition.* Our deepest intentions.

○ *Collective consciousness.* The people who surround us.

The Buddha taught people to think about being mindful of their diet for each type of nutriment. Just like how the edible foods we consume affect the health of our body, everything we allow into our mind through our senses affects our mental health, and so on.

THE FOUR NUTRIMENTS

1. Edible Food: Nourishment for the Body and Mind

The most obvious type of food is what we eat and drink. Our bodies rely on food for energy, and because the body and mind are not separate, the quality of our food also influences our mental and emotional states. Those who have experienced trauma may turn to food for comfort, sometimes engaging in unconscious patterns of emotional eating to soothe distress. Alternatively, trauma can manifest in patterns of food restriction or neglect, reflecting a disconnection from the body's needs.

Mindful eating can be part of reclaiming a sense of safety and presence. Choosing nourishing foods, slowing down while eating, and expressing gratitude for the meal can help reconnect us to the present moment. Trauma often makes us feel disconnected from our bodies, but by bringing awareness to what we consume, we can begin to restore that connection and offer ourselves care and healing.

2. Sensory Impressions: What We Take in Shapes Our Reality

In Buddhism, we talk about the normal five senses of sight, hearing, smell, taste, and touch, and we add one more, which is the sense that perceives thoughts. We describe these six senses as doorways into the mind.

When you watch a scary movie, you are welcoming those images and sounds through the doors of sight and hearing into your mind where they leave an impression. If you spend most of your time exposing yourself to news stories about catastrophe and cruelty, you can think of that as a kind of food you're feeding your mind. It's the same for other senses, including the thoughts you think.

Looking at sense impressions as a form of food invites us to ask: "What would be a healthy diet of sense impressions for me? What kinds of media, conversations, and other experiences would be supportive for my journey of healing trauma?"

Without awareness, we may unknowingly feed our suffering by immersing ourselves in harmful sensory input. Violent entertainment, toxic relationships, and even overstimulation can keep our nervous system in a heightened state of alert. Mindful consumption of sensory input means choosing experiences that nurture safety and peace. Surrounding ourselves with kindness, engaging with nature, and seeking out uplifting conversations can help rewire the brain toward healing rather than reinforcing past pain.

3. Volition: The Direction of Our Healing

Volition, or deep aspiration, acts as the guiding force behind our actions. For those who have experienced trauma, volition can sometimes be shaped by pain rather than by clarity. If past wounds remain unhealed, they may drive us toward seeking control, avoiding vulnerability, or engaging in patterns that feel familiar but don't serve our well-being.

Recognizing the role of volition allows us to assess whether our motivations arise from our seed of suffering or from our deeper values. When our volition is conditioned by trauma, we may find ourselves drawn to environments or relationships that reinforce old wounds. However, by cultivating self-awareness, we can shift our volition toward true healing. We can ask ourselves: "Am I making this choice out of fear, or from my deepest-held values?" Aligning our aspirations with self-compassion rather than reactivity enables us to break free from cycles of suffering.

4. Consciousness: The Collective and Individual Mind

In Buddhism, we say that the nature of mind is dual and permeable. In this sense, *permeable* means that the people and places that surround us soak into our minds like a sponge. *Dual* means that in every interaction, both people are impacted by the other.

In this sense, trauma is not only individual—it's also part of our collective consciousness. Both our pain and our joy, as well as the way we see ourselves and the world, is all influenced by the people around us, the cultural narratives we absorb, and the inherited beliefs we carry. If we live in an environment where fear, anger, and disconnection are prevalent, those emotions become part of our internal landscape. We absorb suffering not only from our own experiences but from the collective energy surrounding us.

Healing from trauma requires actively cultivating a different kind of consciousness. This can mean seeking out relationships that support our growth, engaging in communities that prioritize mindfulness and compassion, and stepping away from environments that reinforce despair. We can choose to nourish the seeds of resilience, hope, and connection within us by surrounding ourselves with people and ideas that align with healing rather than reinforcing pain.

BREAKING FREE: TRANSFORMING THE SEED OF TRAUMA

If trauma continues to thrive in us, it's often because we are unknowingly feeding it. Awareness is the key to change. By identifying the sources of nutriment that sustain our suffering, we can begin to shift toward practices that nourish healing instead.

To transform the seed of trauma, we can:

○ *Practice mindful eating.* Bringing awareness and a spiritual dimension to what we consume, ensuring that we are nourishing ourselves in ways that support both physical and emotional well-being.

○ *Choose our sensory input wisely.* Limiting exposure to media and interactions that reinforce suffering while prioritizing experiences that cultivate safety and joy.

○ *Clarify our volition.* Regularly reflecting on whether our actions stem from old wounds or from a genuine desire for peace and healing.

○ *Engage with a supportive community.* Finding people and spaces that encourage transformation, understanding, and growth.

The seed of trauma, like all seeds, requires food to grow. By becoming mindful of what we consume—through the four types of nutriments—we gain the power to weaken the hold of suffering. The Buddha's teaching on the four nutriments provides a clear path for identifying and transforming what feeds our pain.

32

GETTING TO KNOW SUFFERING
ACCEPTANCE

Every human being suffers. No one who's ever lived has been a stranger to suffering. This is one of the most foundational teachings of Buddhism. Just as night follows day and winter follows summer, suffering and happiness exist together. To seek a life free from suffering is to misunderstand the nature of existence. Instead, the path to peace lies in learning how to hold our suffering with wisdom and compassion.

SEEING THE FLOWER IN THE COMPOST

The teachings of Thich Nhat Hanh remind us that suffering is not something to be discarded or ignored. No matter how smelly and rotten the garbage of life can be, a good gardener will not run away from it. Instead, they know how to transform it into compost, and then transform that compost into flowers and vegetables.

If you look deeply into the flower, you can see it's made of garbage. If you look deeply into the garbage, you can see its potential to become a flower. We can learn to work skillfully with our suffering and transform it into wisdom and compassion. Suffering, when met with mindfulness and care, becomes the raw material for our deepest growth.

THE FUNCTION OF SUFFERING

Suffering is often seen as something to be eliminated, but in reality it serves a vital function. Without suffering, we would not have the capacity for true compassion. The greatest teachers of love and understanding are often those who've known deep pain. Thich Nhat Hanh teaches that just as lotus flowers can only grow in mud, our happiness and wisdom are nurtured by the suffering we transform.

The key to this transformation is our attitude toward suffering. If we reject it, push it away, or try to suppress it, it only becomes more entrenched—it festers. But if we hold suffering with compassion—recognizing that it's a natural part of life—we create the conditions for healing. Instead of seeing suffering as something that defines us, we can learn to see it as something that nourishes us.

TURNING GARBAGE INTO FLOWERS

One of the greatest obstacles to healing is the belief that suffering is worthless. But suffering is not a mistake; it is part of life's natural cycle. The hardships we endure, if met with awareness, become the very material from which we grow stronger and wiser.

It can be helpful to reflect on past struggles and recognize the ways they have shaped you. How has a difficult experience deep-

ened your compassion? In what ways has pain helped you understand others better? Even if you can't find ways that your pain has
become strength, reflect on how it could. If we approach suffering
with curiosity instead of resistance, we begin to see its hidden gifts.

PRACTICAL STEPS FOR TRANSFORMATION

1. *Acknowledge your suffering.* Do not deny or suppress pain.
   Recognize it as it arises and bring awareness to it.

2. *Hold it with kindness.* Instead of pushing suffering away,
   gently embrace it. This can be done through mindful
   breathing or placing a hand on your heart.

3. *See it as compost.* Remind yourself that just as organic
   waste nourishes new growth, your suffering can deepen
   your understanding and compassion.

4. *Water the seeds of joy.* Even while tending to suffering, actively
   nourish the conditions for happiness. Enjoy a simple
   pleasure, connect with a loved one, or appreciate nature.

HOLDING SUFFERING WITH GENTLENESS

Suffering is not a mistake or a failure—it is an inevitable part of
being human. However, our usual reaction is to resist it, to push it
away or try to suppress it. This resistance only intensifies our pain.
Instead, we practice holding our suffering with the same tenderness we would offer to a crying baby. When an infant cries, we don't

scold or abandon them. We hold them close, offering warmth and reassurance. This is the way we must learn to hold our suffering—with kindness, patience, and a willingness to listen.

When suffering arises, we can say to ourselves:

○ "I see you, suffering. I am here for you."

○ "It's okay to feel this. I will take care of you."

○ "I don't need to push this away. I can hold it with love."

By practicing this deep acceptance, we transform our relationship with pain. We begin to see suffering not as an enemy but as a teacher.

BREATHING THROUGH SUFFERING

One of the most powerful resources for embracing suffering is the breath. When difficult emotions arise, the breath can serve as an anchor, keeping us steady in the present moment. Instead of being swept away by fear, anger, or grief, we return to the simple act of breathing.

Try This Practice

1. Close your eyes and take a deep breath in.

2. As you breathe out, imagine releasing tension from your body.

3. With each inhale, say silently, "Breathing in, I acknowledge my suffering."

4. With each exhale, say, "Breathing out, I send myself love and compassion."

With time, this practice allows us to sit with suffering without becoming overwhelmed by it. The breath reminds us that everything is impermanent, including our pain.

TRANSFORMING SUFFERING INTO COMPASSION

When we embrace suffering instead of resisting it, something profound happens: We develop greater compassion for ourselves and others. Our suffering connects us to the suffering of all beings. We begin to see that we are not alone in our struggles, and this recognition fosters deep empathy.

When someone experiences great loss, it can cause them to close their heart or to open it. If we resist grief, we become more closed and disconnected. But when we allow ourselves to feel it fully, we develop the habit of responding to all grief with loving-presence. We also gain insight into the grief of others, become more open, more understanding, and more capable of offering comfort. We are taking the garbage of life and turning it into fresh compost, from which flowers can emerge.

MAINTAINING HOPE IN TIMES OF DESPAIR

Perhaps one of the greatest challenges of deep acceptance is maintaining hope. When suffering feels relentless, it's easy to fall into despair. But Buddhist teachings remind us that everything is impermanent. No matter how intense the suffering, it will change.

During times of war and great hardship, my teacher Thich Nhat Hanh was often asked if peace would ever be possible. His response was always rooted in the reality of impermanence: "Everything changes. If suffering is here now, it will not last forever." This simple truth can sustain us when hope feels distant.

FINDING SUPPORT IN COMMUNITY

While suffering is part of human life, we are not meant to bear it alone. One of the greatest sources of healing is community—being surrounded by people who practice deep listening, understanding, and love.

In Buddhist tradition, the Sangha, or spiritual community, provides a refuge for those who seek peace. When we practice with others, we draw on collective strength. When we're surrounded by people making destructive choices, we become more likely to follow their example. Conversely, if we can surround ourselves with people who prioritize kindness and healing, it becomes so much easier to follow that path.

Consider how you might find more support. A trusted friend, a meditation group, or a compassionate teacher can offer presence and guidance. Sometimes, just knowing that someone is there, holding space for you, can bring profound relief.

THE PATH OF ACCEPTANCE

Deep acceptance of suffering does not mean resignation. It doesn't mean giving up or refusing to work toward change. Rather, it means learning to see suffering as part of life's fabric, holding it with compassion rather than resistance.

The more we practice this acceptance, the more we discover an unexpected freedom. We no longer waste energy fighting what is inevitable. Instead, we cultivate the ability to be with whatever arises, knowing that within every moment of suffering lies the potential for understanding, love, and transformation.

33

A TIME YOU
NEEDED LOVE
TRANSFORMING

Each of us carries moments from our past when we felt alone, unseen, or unloved. These experiences, even if long behind us, remain present in the patterns of the neural networks in our brains. They exist not as distant history but as implicit memories, shaping how we feel, think, and react in the present. In this practice, we don't seek to change what happened but we change how these experiences live inside us. By giving our past self the love and understanding we needed, the memory we carry into the present is transformed.

CHOOSING A MOMENT

Begin by choosing a moment from your past—a time when you needed love and didn't receive it. It might be a time of rejection, loneliness, or misunderstanding. It could be a childhood experience, an adolescent struggle, or even something from adulthood. Choose something meaningful but not overwhelming. A moment that feels alive but not unmanageable. As you get better at this practice, you'll be able to choose more painful memories.

SEEING YOUR PAST SELF

Close your eyes and bring that past self into your mind's eye. See them as clearly as possible. Where are they? What are they feeling? What is happening around them? Notice the emotions on their face, the posture of their body. Try to feel what they're feeling. Let yourself fully acknowledge their pain, confusion, and loneliness.

As you sit with this image, recognize that your past self did not deserve to suffer alone. They were doing the best they could with the resources they had. And now, you—the person you have become—can offer them what they need.

OFFERING LOVE AND UNDERSTANDING

Imagine yourself stepping into the scene. You are there, fully present, ready to offer support. What does your past self need most in this moment? Is it protection, comfort, reassurance? What words would have helped them? What presence would have soothed them?

There are many ways to bring love into this moment:

○ *Your present self intervening.* Imagine walking up to your past self, kneeling down, and saying, "I see you. You are not alone. You are deeply loved." If something harmful is happening, picture yourself stepping in and stopping it.

Imagine holding your younger self's hand or embracing them, letting them know they're safe now.

○ *A loving figure appearing.* If offering love directly feels difficult, you can bring in a figure that represents deep compassion. It might be a spiritual teacher, a loving family member, a pet, or someone who embodies kindness. Picture them sitting beside your past self, offering warmth and protection. What would they say? What presence do they bring?

○ *The most skillful response.* What would have been the most healing, most helpful way for someone to have treated you in that moment? What would have truly soothed and supported you? Imagine that response happening now. Let yourself absorb it fully.

LETTING IT SINK IN

Take time to sit with this visualization. Let your past self feel the presence of love. Notice if anything shifts in your body. Maybe there is a softening in your chest, a loosening in your shoulders, or your breathing feels a bit deeper than before.

This practice is not fantasy or wishful thinking. It is real. The past exists in the present, encoded in your brain and body. By bringing love to these memories and demonstrating how you deserved to be treated, you are not changing history but you are changing how these experiences live inside you now. The neural connections of pain and isolation can be rewired with warmth and care.

RETURNING TO THE PRESENT

When you feel ready, bring your attention back to the present moment. Open your eyes. Feel the weight of your body, the breath in your lungs. Know that the love you offered your past self is real, and that it lives within you now.

Each time you return to this practice, you reinforce new pathways of self-compassion. You show yourself that it is never too late to be loved in the way you always deserved. And as this love grows within, it changes not just the past but the way you move through the world today.

34

A VISIT FROM
YOUR FUTURE SELF
TRANSFORMING

Trauma doesn't disappear. It is not something that fades into the past and vanishes. Instead, it remains within us as a powerful form of emergency learning, shaping how we move through the world. Healing doesn't mean forgetting—it means that the impact of the experience has changed. It no longer distorts the present. Instead, it has become a source of strength, resilience, or deeper compassion for others.

One way to cultivate this transformation is to visualize a visit from your future self. Imagine yourself 10 or 20 years from now, having integrated and healed from your most difficult experiences. This version of you has lived with wisdom and has found ways to face painful experiences without being defined by them. They know what it means to suffer, and they know what it means to heal.

CONNECTING WITH YOUR FUTURE SELF

Find a quiet space and take a few deep breaths. Allow yourself to settle into your body. When you're ready, close your eyes and picture yourself many years from now. This version of you is not perfect, and they are not free from struggle—but they have grown in ways that you may not yet be able to see.

What do they look like? How do they carry themselves? Notice the steadiness in their eyes, the softness in their face. Imagine them coming to visit you as you are now. See them sitting with you, offering their presence.

RECEIVING THEIR MESSAGE

What would your future self want to say to you? What words of encouragement, reassurance, or wisdom do they have? Perhaps they remind you that healing is not about erasing the past but about changing your relationship to it. Maybe they tell you that you are already on the path of transformation, even if it doesn't always feel that way.

If your trauma made you feel isolated, your future self might remind you that you are deeply connected to others. If your trauma made you doubt your worth, they may tell you about the ways you will learn to love yourself more fully. If your trauma has left you feeling unsafe, they might share how you find new ways to trust and create a sense of home in the world.

Listen to their words. Feel their presence. Let yourself absorb what they offer, even if you don't fully believe it yet.

EXAMPLES OF TRANSFORMATION

1. A Childhood of Neglect Becomes a Commitment to Care

Imagine someone who grew up feeling unseen, and their needs ignored. They carry the pain of that neglect into adulthood, which manifests as self-doubt or difficulty trusting others. But through healing, their future self becomes someone who offers deep, unwavering presence to others. Perhaps they are a loving parent, a mentor, or simply someone who takes the time to make others feel valued. They remind you that your pain can give you the ability to care in ways that others may not understand.

2. A Survivor of Violence Finds Their Own Strength

Someone who has lived through violence may have once felt powerless. Fear may have shaped how they moved through the world. But their future self knows that healing has made them strong. They remind you that every time you choose to stand up for yourself, or to be the ally of someone in need, you are rewriting the impact of what happened.

3. Loss Transforms Into a Source of Compassion

Loss, whether of a loved one, a home, or a dream, can leave an ache that feels unbearable. But your future self has found ways to carry that loss with love. Perhaps they have turned their grief into a way to connect with others, to support those who are also struggling. They remind you that even though the pain has not disappeared, it has become part of something larger: a deepened ability to love.

HOLDING THIS VISION

Take a few moments to sit with the presence of your future self. Notice how it feels in your body. What emotions arise? If doubt or skepticism come up, that's okay. This practice is not about forcing belief—it's about planting the seed of possibility. The more you visit this version of yourself, the more you allow that future to shape you in the present.

When you are ready, take a deep breath and slowly bring your awareness back to the room. Open your eyes. Know that your future self is always there, waiting for you to listen. The wisdom you long for is already within you, growing each time you choose to meet yourself with kindness and curiosity.

35

TRANSFORMING
VIOLENCE AND FEAR
SUTRA STUDY

The Buddha's teachings on transforming violence and fear offer profound insights into the healing of trauma. Trauma, at its core, is an imprint of fear and pain left in the mind and body, shaping how we respond to the world. The sutra on transforming violence and fear (*Attadaṇḍa Sutta*), as preserved in Buddhist tradition, provides a framework for meeting trauma with mindfulness, compassion, and deep understanding.

UNDERSTANDING THE ROOTS
OF FEAR AND VIOLENCE

The discourse teaches that violence and fear arise from misunderstanding, ignorance, and suffering. When we are hurt, it's natural to respond with avoidance, anger, or fear to protect ourselves. However, despite being natural ways to respond, they can also deepen our suffering. This is true both in how we treat others and in how we treat ourselves. When we've lived through a traumatic experience, we may internalize self-judgment, shame, or numbing avoidance.

Healing from trauma begins with recognizing that our suffering is not a personal failing but a continuation of suffering that has been transmitted through generations. We carry the pain of those before us, just as they carried the pain of those before them. Understanding this allows us to step out of cycles of self-blame and see our trauma with a wider lens of compassion.

MINDFULNESS AS A TOOL
FOR TRANSFORMATION

The sutra emphasizes the practice of mindfulness as a way to transform suffering. Mindfulness allows us to see our pain clearly without becoming consumed by it. Instead of repressing traumatic memories or becoming overwhelmed by them, we learn to hold them gently, acknowledging their presence while cultivating stability in the present moment.

A core practice from the sutra involves breathing with awareness:

○ "Breathing in, I know that fear is in me."

○ "Breathing out, I hold this fear with compassion."

With each breath, we recognize our suffering and offer it tenderness rather than rejection. This simple yet profound practice can change our relationship with fear. Rather than being something to flee from, it becomes something in need of our care and soothing.

PRACTICING DEEP LISTENING AND COMPASSION FOR OURSELVES

A key teaching from the discourse is the practice of deep listening—not just toward others but toward ourselves. Trauma often leaves us feeling isolated or disconnected from our inner experience. We may fear confronting our pain because we expect it to be unbearable. However, when we approach it with the same deep listening we'd offer a suffering friend, we create a safe space for healing.

Imagine sitting with your younger self, the version of you that endured trauma. Instead of trying to fix, silence, or explain away their pain, simply listen. Let them speak. Let their emotions be expressed. This practice allows us to reconnect with the wounded parts of ourselves that have been ignored or suppressed.

TRANSFORMING THE ENERGY OF TRAUMA WITH LOVING-KINDNESS

The discourse teaches that anger, fear, and other forms of suffering are energies that can be transformed but not destroyed. Just as compost can nourish a garden, our suffering can be used to cultivate wisdom and compassion. One of the most powerful ways to do this is through *metta* (loving-kindness) practice:

○ "May I be safe."

○ "May I be free from suffering."

○ "May I be at peace."

Repeating these phrases while holding your trauma with awareness begins the process of transformation. The suffering does not disappear overnight but over time, the way it resides in your mind and body changes. It no longer feels like a weight that controls you—instead, it becomes part of your story, integrated with love and wisdom.

BREAKING THE CYCLE OF TRAUMA

One of the discourse's most profound insights is that when we heal ourselves, we heal those who came before us and those who will come after us. Violence and fear are passed down through generations but so is healing. When we choose to meet our trauma with compassion rather than repression or retaliation, we are interrupting the cycle. This is a radical act of transformation—not just for ourselves but for the collective suffering of humanity.

By practicing mindfulness, deep listening, and loving-kindness, we rewrite the impact of trauma. We shift from being victims of our past to being caretakers of our present. The seeds of violence and fear that were planted in us can be transformed, just as the Buddha taught, into seeds of understanding, resilience, and peace.

36

THREE DOORS
OF LIBERATION
SUTRA STUDY

The *Discourse on the Dharma Seal: The Three Doors of Liberation* offers profound insight into the nature of reality and freedom. These teachings—emptiness, signlessness, and aimlessness—are traditionally used to break through attachment and suffering. When applied to trauma healing, they provide a path to move beyond pain, reshape our perceptions, and cultivate deep inner liberation.

EMPTINESS: RELEASING THE
SOLID SELF OF TRAUMA

In Buddhist teachings, emptiness (*sunyata*) doesn't mean that things don't exist. It means that everything exists in relationship, without a separate, independent self. Trauma can feel like it defines us, as if we are permanently shaped by our worst experiences. We may carry the belief that *I am broken, I will always suffer,* or *I cannot be whole.*

Through the practice of emptiness, we begin to see that our suffering is not a fixed identity. The pain we experience is real, but it is not who we are. Just as a wave is not separate from the ocean, we are not separate from the causes and conditions that shaped us. And just as the wave changes form, so too can our relationship to trauma evolve.

To apply this, when painful memories arise, we can remind ourselves: *Causes and conditions are creating the experience of suffering right now. It is not a permanent, separate self. I am more than my trauma.* This shift in perspective creates space for healing by loosening the rigid stories we tell about our pain.

SIGNLESSNESS: LETTING GO OF FIXED PERCEPTIONS

Signlessness (*animitta*) invites us to look beyond appearances. When we experience trauma, we often assign fixed meanings to what happened—believing that we are doomed to repeat the past, that others will always harm us, or that safety is unattainable. These rigid perceptions keep us stuck, reacting to present situations based on past wounds.

Practicing signlessness means seeing beyond our conditioned views. When we look at a cloud, it might seem obvious that it is a cloud and nothing else. However, looking in this way can blind us to a deeper understanding. A cloud is not only a cloud—it is made of water, air, and heat. Looking deeply, we can see that the presence of those elements are present in the cloud. When we're willing to look deeper, we can see that meanings we thought were obvious and complete might actually be missing something.

Our trauma is also not a fixed, unchangeable thing. It has layers, context, and the potential to transform. In meditation, we can reflect: "What if my trauma doesn't mean what I think it does? What would it mean if I knew I've always been lovable?" This practice softens our grip on suffering and allows for new possibilities to emerge.

AIMLESSNESS: STOPPING THE CHASE FOR COMPLETION

Trauma often leaves us with a sense that something is missing—that we must *fix* ourselves, find closure, or reach a state where we no longer feel pain. Aimlessness (*apranihita*) teaches that we do not need to become something else to be whole. Freedom is found in stopping the chase and fully arriving in the present moment.

This doesn't mean giving up on healing but rather releasing the belief that we must *achieve* something in order to be at peace. Instead of thinking, "I will be free when my trauma is gone," we shift to "I can experience freedom even as I hold my pain with compassion."

To practice this, we can sit in meditation and say, "There is nowhere to go, nothing to become. Right now, in this moment, I have everything I need to heal."

INTEGRATING THE THREE DOORS IN HEALING

Healing from trauma is not about erasing the past but about transforming our relationship to it. Through *emptiness*, we see that our suffering is not a fixed identity. Through *signlessness*, we release rigid stories that keep us trapped. Through *aimlessness*, we stop running from ourselves and embrace the present as it is.

Each time we touch these insights, we can experience a moment of liberation—not just from past pain but from the way suffering shapes our experience of the present. This is the path to deep, enduring healing.

37

TRAUMA AS FUEL
FOR CHANGE
COMPASSIONATE ACTION

My teacher, Thich Nhat Hanh, was born in Vietnam and spent much of his young life trying to stop the war between his country and the United States. He was eventually exiled from Vietnam because he refused to take a side. He was a voice for peace.

Decades later, he held a meditation retreat for veterans from both sides of that war. During a question-and-answer segment, an American veteran approached him in total despair.

His voice was heavy with shame as he told the story of coming to a village in Vietnam and setting a trap. He placed plastic explosives in a bag filled with sandwiches in the center of the village, and then hid in the jungle. To his horror, he saw a group of small children find the sandwiches, open the bag, and all of them were killed. He said, "Since that day, I've never been able to be in the same room as children. How can I ever practice with this? How can I ever forgive myself?" He had seen too much, done things he could not undo, and lived every day with the weight of what had happened.

For years, his trauma had consumed him. The faces of those children appeared in his dreams. He carried their voices in his mind, a chorus of ghosts he couldn't silence. He had come to believe that his suffering was a punishment, something he was doomed to bear. He felt there was nothing left for him but regret.

Thich Nhat Hanh listened carefully, his presence calm and unwavering. Then he said something no one could have expected. He said, "It's not too late to save those children." Everyone in the room held their breath. How could that be? They were already gone.

Thich Nhat Hanh continued, "Every day, children die for lack of a little food or medicine. If you want to, you could save the lives of 20 children each day for the rest of your life." The veteran sat in stunned silence. For so long, he had been living in the past, trapped in what could not be changed. But now, for the first time, he saw another path. If his pain had been caused by taking life, perhaps his healing could come from saving it.

TRANSFORMING PAIN INTO PURPOSE

This conversation changed everything for him. Instead of being swallowed by shame, he began using his trauma as fuel for action. He dedicated himself to humanitarian work, helping children in war-torn and impoverished areas. Each life he touched became a form of atonement—not in a way that erased his past but in a way that gave it meaning. He was still carrying his trauma, but now it had direction. Instead of paralyzing him, it propelled him forward.

This story is a powerful reminder that suffering does not have to define us. Trauma can feel like it has taken everything from us—our sense of safety, our self-worth, our belief in goodness. But sometimes, that same suffering can become the force that moves us toward healing, not just for ourselves but for others.

A REFLECTION PRACTICE: FINDING THE PATH FORWARD

If you are carrying trauma that feels too heavy to bear, take a moment to reflect. Find a quiet space, take a few breaths, and consider the following:

1. What has your pain taught you about suffering?
   - Has it made you more sensitive to others who struggle? Has it shown you where healing is needed in the world?

2. How could your suffering be transformed into service?
   - Could your experience help others who have been through similar hardships? Could it inspire you to create something—art, writing, community—that brings light to others?

3. What is one small step you can take?
   - Transformation doesn't have to be grand. A single kind action, a moment of listening, a choice to help— each of these is a step toward turning pain into purpose.

As Thich Nhat Hanh said, "It's not too late." Whatever has happened in your life, whatever suffering you carry, there is still something you can do. Your trauma is part of your story, but it does not have to be the end of it. The pain that once seemed unbearable may one day become the reason someone else finds hope.

INDEX

ABOUT THE AUTHOR

Tim Desmond is a psychotherapist, meditation teacher, and Distinguished Faculty Scholar at Antioch University. A longtime student of Zen Master Thich Nhat Hanh, he is the founder of Peer Collective, and cofounder of Morning Sun Mindfulness Center. He lives in Santa Cruz, CA, and teaches Buddhist practices to audiences around the world. His publications include *Self-Compassion in Psychotherapy* (Norton, 2015), *The Self-Compassion Skills Workbook* (Norton, 2017), and *How to Stay Human in a F*cked Up World* (HarperOne, 2019).